The Essential Guide to Doing the School Play

The Essential Guide to Doing the School Play

And Not Screwing It Up

Jason Hanlan

methuen | drama
LONDON • NEW YORK • OXFORD • NEW DELHI • SYDNEY

METHUEN DRAMA

Bloomsbury Publishing Plc, 50 Bedford Square, London, WC1B 3DP, UK
Bloomsbury Publishing Inc, 1359 Broadway, New York, NY 10018, USA
Bloomsbury Publishing Ireland, 29 Earlsfort Terrace, Dublin 2, D02 AY28, Ireland

BLOOMSBURY, METHUEN DRAMA and the Methuen Drama logo are trademarks of
Bloomsbury Publishing Plc

First published in Great Britain 2026

Copyright © Jason Hanlan, 2026

Jason Hanlan has asserted his right under the Copyright, Designs and Patents Act, 1988, to
be identified as Author of this work.

For legal purposes the Acknowledgements on p. x constitute an extension of this
copyright page.

Cover design by Ben Anslow

All rights reserved. No part of this publication may be: i) reproduced or transmitted
in any form, electronic or mechanical, including photocopying, recording or by means
of any information storage or retrieval system without prior permission in writing
from the publishers; or ii) used or reproduced in any way for the training,
development or operation of artificial intelligence (AI) technologies, including
generative AI technologies. The rights holders expressly reserve this publication
from the text and data mining exception as per Article 4(3) of the
Digital Single Market Directive (EU) 2019/790.

Bloomsbury Publishing Plc does not have any control over, or responsibility for,
any third-party websites referred to or in this book. All internet addresses given in
this book were correct at the time of going to press. The author and publisher
regret any inconvenience caused if addresses have changed or sites have
ceased to exist, but can accept no responsibility for any such changes.

A catalogue record for this book is available from the British Library.

A catalog record for this book is available from the Library of Congress.

ISBN: HB: 978-1-3505-0177-5
PB: 978-1-3505-0176-8
ePDF: 978-1-3505-0178-2
eBook: 978-1-3505-0179-9

Typeset by RefineCatch Limited, Bungay, Suffolk
Printed and bound in Great Britain

For product safety related questions contact productsafety@bloomsbury.com.

To find out more about our authors and books visit www.bloomsbury.com
and sign up for our newsletters.

CONTENTS

About this book vii
A bit about me ix
Acknowledgements x
Introduction 1

1. What is a school production? 7
2. The right order 9
3. The right stuff 13
4. What's out there? 27
5. Selling it to the boss 55
6. Selling it to the students 61
7. Performing rights and permissions 65
8. Visions and venues 71
9. Putting your team together 77
10. Directors and directing 85
11. Musical directors and choreographers 89
12. Designing and making your set and props 99
13. Money stuff and front of house 105
14. Sound and light and all things technical 113
15. Stage managing 121
16. Costumes, make-up and hair 127
17. Your cast and their parents 135

18 Timescales, lists and schedules 141

19 Auditions and casting 147

20 The first cast and crew meeting 157

21 Rehearsing 161

22 The language of the theatre 167

23 A collection of minor disasters 169

24 How it played out 175

25 A shout-out for Shakespeare! 183

26 'So, what are we doing next?' 189

Appendices 193

ABOUT THIS BOOK

Theatre is a community: a collective act of creation where no director stands alone. This book is about building a community, a team that brings a production to life.

Sooner or later in their career, the drama teacher will be expected to produce a school play. But this doesn't only apply to the trained drama teacher. In many centres, this duty can fall upon the English department, the music teacher or a PE/dance teacher. The task is, more often than not, underestimated; in particular, when volunteered for, or bestowed upon, a busy newly qualified teacher (NQT)/early career teacher (ECT), no matter what their specialism. Teacher training equips specialists to become effective theatre educators; however, this should not be mistaken for the diverse skills required to produce and direct a full school play.

This is my third book for drama teachers and it provides a complete step-by-step guide to the enormous task of putting together and producing a successful school production, no matter what your specialism. It is essential for those new to school shows and an extremely useful aid to the more experienced. Included are twenty-six informative chapters which break down and describe in detail the process of page to stage, with examples from all-time favourite blockbusters such as *Grease* and *Oliver!* to less well-known straight plays and comedies. Throughout the book, I will share the thoughts and insights of sixteen different, exceptional people who have been involved with me in a school play in one role or another. These trusted voices will reflect upon their vast experiences as: director, musical director, stage manager, sound/lighting technician, designer/artist, set/props builder, wardrobe, make-up, front of house, choreographer, parent or performer.

This book aims to provide all you will need to produce and direct a memorable and successful school show, including a valuable chapter on how to manage the finances of the show and, most importantly, stay sane. Throughout the book, I have sprinkled **warnings** which are based on real-life mistakes, errors and catastrophes experienced by myself or close colleagues. I share them so that you will not have to. The book offers 'pros and cons' considerations in order to foster a balanced debate.

Some concepts in this book naturally overlap or reappear in multiple sections. This repetition is intentional, serving as a way to reinforce key ideas and support the director's learning, given the wealth of information to take in. Additionally, certain points are reiterated because this book is designed as a practical resource for teachers; a guide to be dipped into as needed, rather than read cover-to-cover in one sitting.

At the end of the book, there is an appendix featuring seven useful information sheets, glossaries, sample letters and contracts that are referenced throughout the text.

A BIT ABOUT ME

I qualified as a drama teacher in 1994, and went on to teach in two large comprehensives in the UK, as head of drama and, later, performing arts. Along the way, I worked as a local education authority advisor for drama and a teacher trainer. Alongside teaching, I worked as a senior moderator/examiner for fifteen years. Mostly though, for the last twenty-eight years, I've been a drama teacher in British secondary schools and, more recently, internationally. I now live in Mendoza, Argentina, where I was Profesor de Teatro at Colegio Las Candelas Mendoza Argentina for five years. I am currently Asesor Académico del Programa de Arte de la Universidad Congreso. (Academic Consultant for the Arts at Congreso University, Argentina).

My first book, *200 Plays for GCSE and A-Level Performance,* published by Methuen in 2021, is used extensively as a resource for drama teachers seeking the best published materials for their students. My second book, *200 Themes For Devising With 11–18 Year Olds*, was published by Methuen in 2024 and was a finalist for the Outstanding Drama Education Resource category in the Music and Drama Education Awards 2025.

ACKNOWLEDGEMENTS

Anna Brewer, Publisher for Methuen Drama at Bloomsbury, who envisioned three books for teachers where I saw only one, and guided my steps accordingly.

Special thanks to my sixteen friends and colleagues, who contributed their thoughts and expertise in their chosen fields.

Mark Lovejoy: director
Debbie Coad: director
Jennie Pitman: musical director
Gwawr Mills: musical director
Kirsty Edwards-Longhurst: choreographer
Nikki Dobbs: choreographer
Jonathan Hamblin: set designer and artist
Janette Anderson: front of house
Stuart Mantle: technician (sound and light)
Benjamin Hanlan: technician (sound and light)
Helen Maree: stage manager
Joan Wilcox: wardrobe
Norma Cockcroft: hair and make-up
Chanel Waddock: actor/artist
Heather Pugsley: parent and volunteer
Alethea Truin: parent governor

A special mention to all the groups out there on social media who come together to support, advise and help teachers make school theatre for kids all over the world.

For Monica. Wife, publicist and social media guru.

Introduction

The magic of a school play lies in its many facets. It goes beyond mere entertainment; it's a transformative experience that nurtures vital life skills such as collaboration, teamwork and resilience. A school play isn't just an extracurricular activity; it's an essential component of an education that equips students for success both on and off the stage.

Putting on a school show is a demanding – at times gruelling, nerve shredding, testing and utterly exhausting – experience. It is also, without question and by far, the most exhilarating, fulfilling, rewarding endeavour this drama teacher was ever a part of in his teaching career.

In over twenty-eight years, I have directed/produced more than forty shows; from all-singing, all-dancing musicals to small intimate studio performances, and each one has been a highlight in my career. I am blessed to have been able to work with countless talented and passionate students and their teachers; to have seen the process of page to stage come to life, where students feel that rush of being a part of something special. From the first audition's tears and laughter to that moment when the lights come up and the audience falls silent. I shall miss such work whenever I decide to fold away my director's chair. But there were moments.

Everyone loves a school musical, right?

The terrifying tale of a new teacher's first full-blown school production

I remember it well. Still in my first term, and fresh out of university, I felt it was time to announce my intention to 'do a school play'. Perhaps it was the excitement that comes with the Christmas season in a school, but I was overflowing with energy and goodwill. After all, we had discussed it during the interview and, for some reason, I felt it was a strength. The head was delighted and ushered me into his office that break time, where he informed me that he and his wife met while rehearsing *Sweeney Todd,* the musical; that it was a great show and he would 'help out'. My dreams of putting on

Equus were placed on the back burner and, as I left his office cursing softly to myself, the head's rendition of 'The Worst Pies in London' sounded the first tuneless alarm bells.

I was advised to see the head of music as soon as possible. So I knocked on her door that very afternoon. She was a lovely, helpful woman who told me she was far too busy with the senior choir but that her newly qualified music teacher would love to help. The fresh-out-of-the-box music teacher was as happy to 'help' as I had been to have *Sweeney* thrust upon me! She was so happy in fact, that she took the next three weeks off sick, right up to the end of that terrifying first term.

I researched all I could on *The Sweeney Todd Shock 'n' Roll Show*, and all too soon the forty-one ordered scripts arrived from Samuel French, along with a baffling musical score. The script I understood, although it wasn't Peter Shaffer, but the music was vast and overwhelming. The head, who had become my mentor for this part of my professional development, assured me he would help until the poorly new music teacher returned.

Before we broke up for Christmas, I had advertised for two weeks, in assemblies and on posters, that the school play (corrected by the head in red pen to 'school musical') would be in June and auditions would be taking place in the first week of the spring term. There were 1,200 students at my new school so I was rather disappointed when only nine of them showed an interest. But, once again, the head came to my rescue with a series of 'motivational assemblies' about the 'school ethos' and 'taking part', which magically raised the number interested in auditioning to a pleasing though alarming 180. I had so much to learn!

Over the Christmas holidays, I planned a rehearsal schedule which effectively lengthened my Wednesdays, Thursdays and Fridays by two hours and surrendered Monday, Tuesday and Thursday lunchtimes every week right through until June. I couldn't do Wednesday lunchtimes as I had also volunteered to run the school chess club, and Friday lunchtimes were exam revision. I had cleverly worked out this would give me more than enough time to 'Do a musical'. I worked out that, if I gave a week to the audition process, I could be cast and ready to run by the third week back after the school holidays in January. My calculations even took into consideration half terms and end-of-term holidays. I even remembered Easter Monday!

On 3 January, I announced that auditions would take place after school on Monday 16, Tuesday 17 and Wednesday 18 January. Monday for singers, Tuesday for actors and Wednesday for recalls.

The word went round and Monday 16 January was audition day one. Singers! The new music teacher had 'generously' agreed to come along and help and her idea was to allow students to bring their own prepared 'favourite' song to sing for us. If they wanted, she would accompany them or they could bring their own backing track. The head was true to his word, and turned up to assist. The three of us sat at a desk in the main hall and waited. What followed were 125 minutes which have haunted me ever since.

Karaoke hell would be one way to describe what followed. The students waiting to audition were sat behind us and, even with the head teacher present and perhaps because of their own nerves, they were not the most supportive of audiences. Yes, there were girls who sang like angels and boys who sang like girls. I heard 'Tomorrow' from *Annie* thirteen times that afternoon, along with numerous favourites and popular songs of the moment. At least with each song the crowd behind me grew smaller, yet even they became restless and needed to be threatened with detentions before we could complete the process. One girl in year seven introduced herself by telling us she was going to do some animal impersonations and before we could stop her she launched herself around the stage barking at invisible objects before rapidly and quite slickly moving on to a cow, followed by a duck and some kind of crazed gorilla. She took it very seriously and even the remaining students were stunned into silence. When it was all over, the Head rose rapidly, leaving me with the haunting phrase, 'Well done and good luck!'. The music teacher smiled and told me, as she packed up her sheet music and boom box, that she thought 'Some of them had done really well'. Then she too was gone. The hall was empty and I sat staring at a neat list of perhaps thirty-five names, some with scribbled notes, some that were just blank. I noted that a few had rather tellingly left before it was their turn to embarrass themselves. My silent thoughts were interrupted by the caretaker enquiring whether I had a home to go to.

Day two was the acting audition. There were many of the same faces from Monday and a good number of new, serious contenders. This time I was on my own, the head having explained that his forte was the musical side of things. I did miss his soothing influence over the large group of excited students, but pressed on with what surely was my forte. I used a workshop approach, with a number of improv games, before moving to some brief scripted situations. (Just like I had experienced at uni.) I did identify some fair talent and, from my one term as a teacher at the school, had some ideas already. The perfect boy to play Sweeney couldn't sing, and I mean really couldn't sing. That afternoon they just kept coming and my two hours ran into three, and then the caretaker simply turned off the lights. It seemed everyone loved the idea of Mr Hanlan's first school production. Everyone except the caretaker.

On day three, I was again joined by the music teacher, who informed me she was 'not a lover of musicals'. While I was pondering this, the head 'popped in' to see 'how things were going' and to remind me that the caretaker wanted me out by 5.30 pm.

By 5:35 pm, I had finished. Over three long and exhausting afternoons, I had watched and listened to 117 students and one animal impersonator. Now all I had to do was come up with a cast. For the next four days, including the weekend, I pondered over my scribbled lists and the notes of my two advisors, and drew up a provisional cast list. Some decisions had been obvious, some were a risk worth taking but – apart from having a tone-deaf lead – I was fairly happy with our cast. So, armed with our cast list, I trotted along to the head's office. He was delighted and grabbed it with real enthusiasm. He then gave it careful consideration for roughly eight seconds before asking, 'How many auditioned?' '117', I proudly announced. 'This cast list is for twenty-seven'; 'Yes', I replied quite innocently. And then he hit me with the bombshell: 'Right then! For a school of this size and considering how many auditioned you need to double that figure! Let's say a cast of fifty.'

Now, *The Sweeney Todd Shock 'n' Roll Show* schools edition has twenty named characters plus assorted madhouse keepers and inmates, newsboys, citizens and victims. So, even including Orlando, the Sorcerer's faithful hound (at least I had that part filled), I was going to struggle to give out another twenty-three parts, no matter how inclusive a school we wanted to be.

Then I came up with my most disastrously clever plan to date. I would simply (apart from the two main characters) double-cast the entire musical! The head was delighted and could see I was truly embracing the school ethos. I went home feeling I'd truly found my vocation.

It took one short week to realize that double-casting meant double rehearsal time and I would need to give up Mondays and Tuesdays too, and every lunchtime and about five weekends. Plus attend newly qualified teacher (NQT) courses; complete my NQT's folder of evidence; look after my tutor group; oh, and teach! The nightmare had begun. I had got some things right at least, like securing the performing rights and ordering the scripts and music well in advance; but above all, like the students, I was very keen.

I knew about directing actors and students of theatre but directing a huge double cast, twice, after spending the day in classrooms was, shall we say, very demanding. Then there were the silly things like not being able to use the hall and its stage, or the drama studio to rehearse in for most of May and the whole of June because of the mocks, followed by the exams themselves. There were students off sick, on unauthorized holidays or on school trips; sports day; a football tournament; two exclusions; the fire brigade; torn costumes and obsolete lighting rigs. And then someone asked me if I'd had any thoughts about selling tickets!

More than twenty-five years later, I am ready to talk about it. This book is me talking about it and sharing the experiences of others in the field. It is about what I learned over twenty-eight years, and how 'doing the school play' is still one of the most uplifting, rewarding things a student or teacher can be involved in. The following twenty-five chapters are a step-by-step breakdown of how to do it properly. The first three nights of *Sweeney Todd* were a resounding and very memorable success, but I wish someone had written this book back then.

Let's begin with the essential checklist I wish I'd had!

Who you will need to talk to:

- At the school:
  - Your head teacher/principal and/or senior managers.
  - The site manager/caretaking team.
  - Exams office/coordinator (consult academic calendar).
  - All heads of department/faculty for any event which may clash.
  - Pupils.
  - All staff (recruiting that vital help) whilst being transparent about the commitment of time and energy.
  - See Chapter 9: 'Putting your team together.'
- Out of school:
  - The parents (constant).
  - The governors/academy trustees.
  - The licensing agent for the production.
  - If not from the agent, you will need to obtain scripts and libretto.
  - The fire service (for any productions with a paying/invited audience).
  - Costume/prop equipment rental.
  - Local shops and businesses (potential sponsors/advertisers for your programme/show).
  - Local newspapers/media.

Above all, you'll need to become a true 'problem solver'; someone who can anticipate issues and deal with them as they arise. To do things in the right order (Chapter 2) and ensure everything runs like clockwork (more or less). This book is designed to guide you through that process, time and time again.

1

What is a school production?

My primary school in Wales was well known for its nativity plays, certainly in our valley. The music teacher was a hugely ambitious woman and set herself and the school two impossible goals for the yearly Christmas production: it had to be better than the previous year in every way; but by far the most challenging goal was that it had to involve every child in the school, and 'involve' meant they were 'on stage'. Fortunately, it was a small school so there were only around 160 kids but, being a small school, it also had a rather small stage! Mrs Evans was very traditional, so there was only ever going to be one Mary and one Joseph; she stretched to eight shepherds but firmly limited the wise men to three. There were a couple of other parts on offer, including the owner of the inn and his wife but – as the angel was always played by a teacher and the baby Jesus was a doll – this left around 145 kids with no real reason to be on that tiny stage. But she had an answer to that. Animals! And, being Wales, of course they were singing animals.

Parents – whether out of duty, nostalgia or for sheer amusement – filled the seats, to reminisce about their time on that very stage. It was in fact a huge social event, not to be missed. The spectacle often ended with a comedic flourish as a handful of the smaller 'animals' tumbled off the stage, much to everyone's delight. Admittedly, we only all came on for the final song, but it offered great entertainment. It was indeed 'A whole-school production', annual and very inclusive; in fact, there was no escape.

For many students, teachers and parents, the nativity serves as a debut in the world of school productions, which grows into a love of the theatre. I also acknowledge that for others it serves as a stark reminder to never put yourself in such a situation ever again.

Expectations!

A school show is a tradition; a rite of passage for many. The expectations everyone has of it are indeed 'high fantastical!'. As the director, our expectations of the school play are for nothing short of perfection. We want a production that transcends the ordinary; a true creative masterpiece that showcases the exceptional talent and boundless imaginations of our students. Our dream is to see a performance filled with innovative storytelling, stunning acting and moments that rival those on Broadway and the West End. We want it to receive rapturous standing ovations each night, and for every moment to be unforgettable and leave the audience spellbound. A flawless performance, with ne'er a single forgotten line, missed cue, or technical glitch. We want to see our students grow and shine, demonstrating their remarkable skills as actors, singers and dancers, as well as technicians and musicians. We want glowing reviews and heartfelt praise from the community and local media, celebrating all the hard work and creativity that went into it. That's what we want, right?

The head will want a show that aligns perfectly with their educational goals and showcases the students' learning. The word the head will be looking for is 'excellence', with flawless student conduct on and off the stage reflecting the school's values. The show should boost the school spirit and unity in a smooth operation without a single logistical hiccup. The publicity it receives will obviously need to be very positive and significantly enhance the school's reputation whilst being safe and inclusive, with all students being involved. Of course!

Then there's your cast; they will want to feel like superstars, with their own spotlit moment on stage. They will love building those new friendships and the camaraderie you spoke so much about! The cast and crew will have an absolutely fantastic time from start to finish. They will wear the most amazing, elaborate, epic and dazzling costumes under the greatest lighting imaginable, performing faultlessly before admiring fans, peers, teachers and parents.

Also, their parents and families will love to see their child on stage giving a heart-rending, funny, poignant, professional performance, filling them with unfettered pride! They would like perfect photo opportunities in those epic costumes, or singing that tear-jerking song. What they really want is memories. Sparkling, unforgettable memories.

In a nutshell, you have to create a touch of magic, continue a timeless tradition and bring joy to all. Indeed, the school play is so deeply entrenched in the culture of many schools that we cling to it long after we ourselves leave school. We cling to memories of being a part of it, either in it ourselves or watching our friends on that great school stage. We look back fondly and reminisce. So fond are we, we feel the need to make TV series and movies about it. Movies like *Hunky Dory* and *High School Musical* or series like *Glee*; even *Waterloo Road* took a few episodes out of the troubled lives of its students to cover a school play.

One more thing . . .

A friend of mine once summed up the school play as follows: 'It's about kids doing what they thought they couldn't do.' I firmly believe this is surely what makes all those wild expectations worthwhile.

2

The right order

When I got my first post as a newly qualified drama teacher, the possibility – nay, certainty – of me putting on a school play had already been discussed at interview. In fact, it had been more of a priority than actually teaching my subject! It seemed the school had not produced a play in a number of years and was in need of rekindling its theatre. Backstage had, as in many busy schools, become a storage space for anything broken, lost and unwanted, including approximately 200 chairs. Clearing the performance area should have been on my list of 'Things to do sooner rather than later', but it wasn't. There was after all so much on that list. Stuff like: talking to the bursar, the fire brigade, the caretaker, the licence holder, someone who knew about lighting and sound, someone who could tell me if the hall was booked for any other events, the exams officer, the art teacher, the music teacher, the head teacher, my head of department and, if he was there, Uncle Tom Cobley and all of his team too.

There is an order in which we should attempt most things and putting on a school play is very definitely no exception!

After much trial and error, I finally figured out the best order for planning, perfecting and performing a school play. I'm happy to share this knowledge so others can avoid complete exhaustion, near-madness and major blunders. The first thing you should ask yourself is, 'Am I ready for this?' This is an important consideration for the young, newly qualified and more experienced alike, for there will be times when putting on a school production is simply going to be too much. Try to avoid killer combinations like; whole-school production and moving or new baby. Or big musical and head of music leaving before the production date. Ask yourself, is this the right time? Should I really do this in my first year? If the answer is 'yes', then here is my correct order in which to 'Do the school play'.

1. Assess any available budget (Chapter 13).
2. Consider the school's culture and values (Chapter 3).
3. Evaluate the size and composition of your possible cast. Choose a play with a cast size and character breakdown that suits the number, ability and diversity of your students. A play that will

captivate and entertain. Ensure the play is right for your school and that the senior management will approve of it (Chapter 3).

4. Check that the play is available and you can obtain all the necessary rights and permissions needed to perform it within your time frame. Some licence holders will do this for you but ensure your neighbouring schools are not considering the same play at a similar time (Chapter 7).
5. Consider the venue for such a production (Chapter 8).
6. Book any and all spaces you will require (as far in advance as possible).
7. Put an ad in the school newsletter for staff/parents and other adults who would be interested in assisting the school production. Include a list of roles/skills required.
8. Recruit and assemble a production team to assist with various aspects of the production, such as set design, costumes, lighting, sound and stage management (Chapter 9).
9. Develop a clear vision for the production, including the overall tone, style and interpretation of the play. Consider how you will bring the script to life on stage and communicate your vision to the cast and crew. You should begin to formulate a vision of what you want it to look like (Chapter 8).
10. Logistics and feasibility: assess the logistical feasibility of producing the play within your school's constraints. Consider factors such as rehearsal time, technical requirements and potential scheduling clashes with other school activities. With this and any licensing agreement in mind, you should fix the performance date(s).
11. Hold a meeting for all staff/adults who have expressed a willingness to help/participate. Get your site manager/caretaker/janitor onside with perhaps a role within the process. Involve them. You need them on your team; remember you will represent extra work and headaches for the site team, so you need to make them feel important to the process. Because they will be!
12. Hold a further meeting for all students who are interested in cast/crew positions. At this meeting, you should hand out the audition information pack (Appendix A).
13. Audition and cast (Chapter 19).
14. Create a rehearsal schedule that allows sufficient time for blocking, line learning, character development, and technical rehearsals. Consider the availability of students and any other commitments they may have (Chapter 18).
15. Hold a cast and crew meeting. This is where you can hand out the show packs (Appendix B and Chapter 20).

16. Hold a cast read-through, where notes can be taken and characters/plot discussed. I like to invite everyone involved to this.
17. Technical and design elements: coordinate the design and implementation of technical elements such as set design, lighting, sound, costumes and props. Ensure that these elements enhance the storytelling and create the desired atmosphere.
18. Promotion and publicity: develop a marketing plan to promote the production within the school and community. Consider strategies such as posters, flyers, social media, press releases, and word-of-mouth advertising. Recruit a front of house team (Chapter 13).
19. Maintain a strict rehearsal regime.
20. Run at least one weekend rehearsal just prior to the show itself. I suggest, if possible, to do a full tech run-through on the Saturday and a full dress rehearsal on the Sunday. Try to do two clear runs.
21. The performance area and front of house should be ready by the weekend dress rehearsal, at the latest!
22. Opening night. I run three shows, on Thursday, Friday and Saturday.
23. After the show, carry out post-show checks (Chapter 26).

One more thing . . .

The exact order may vary a little, depending on your school/college and students, but having a plan of action is important and sticking to it is essential.

3

The right stuff

Selecting scripts that best suit your students and school

More than a few years ago now, my sixth-form students and I decided to do a small, intimate studio performance of their studied piece, Wertenbaker's *Our Country's Good*. We had done a whole-school production of *Oliver!* earlier that year, and this was going to be different! Things were going well, when one fine afternoon the head dropped in on a rehearsal. He watched and listened for a few moments before asking the question, 'Do they have to swear?' and, after a moment's thought, 'This is just the sixth form, right?' Without waiting for an answer he went on to enquire as to why I didn't concentrate on, 'Wholesome plays for all the family "like that *Oliver!* you did last term". "Or *Grease?*"'. You know the one; I've done it twice, everyone loves the songs but, wholesome family fun? At that time the play included 'wholesome' themes like; giving in to peer pressure, teenage pregnancy, mooning at passers-by and a casual reference to date rape! And although I love *Oliver!* it is about a gang of criminals who physically abuse women and children; child labour; prostitution; alcohol abuse and murder. So I guess that if you sing about it, anything goes! But, seriously, you have to really think long and hard about what is and what isn't appropriate for your school and your students.

In Chapter 4, 'What's out there?', I list some of the great material available, including *Grease* and *Oliver!* (because they are fantastic). But it isn't only about what suits your school and students; there's also the wider community (your audience) and what any potential cast may want to perform and be capable of performing. You may think you have a textbook cast for *Little Shop of Horrors* but what if they don't want to do a musical?

So, just how do you select the right play for your school and students? Before thinking of casting anything, begin by looking at what you have physically and what may hinder or limit your vision. What I refer to as your resources and constraints.

Resources (what you actually have):

School/college facilities
> Auditorium/theatre: main performance space.
> Classrooms/studio: for rehearsals, meetings, and workshops.
> Equipment: lighting, sound systems, stage props, costumes, and set construction tools.

Human resources
> Students: actors, stage crew and production assistants.
> Teachers: assistance from other teachers/specialists, such as those from the music, art, PE/dance and English departments.
> Parents and volunteers: to help with costumes, sets and fundraising.
> Community members: willing local experts.

Budget
> School funding: allocated budget for arts and extracurricular activities. (If you're lucky.)
> Fundraising: events, sponsorships and donations.
> Grants: applications for arts grants from local or national organizations.

Materials and supplies
> Costumes: existing costumes (check out your storage area), donations.
> Props and set pieces: borrowed, built by students, or simply lying around in your stock cupboard.
> Scripts and music: what existing scripts do you have? Remember, however, that owning the script/music does not give you performance rights.

Constraints (often hidden):

Time (often underestimated!)
> Rehearsal schedule: limited availability due to students' academic commitments.
> Production timeline: deadlines for casting, rehearsals and performance dates.

Budget (often overestimated!)
> Cost management: balancing quality and cost for sets, costumes and technical equipment.
> Fundraising challenges: ensuring enough funds are raised to cover all expenses.

Space limitations
> Availability: limited access to the auditorium or theatre due to other school activities. (For example, the exam season might lay claim to your spaces!)

Size: space constraints for set construction and storage.

Student participation
Experience levels: varied levels of acting and technical experience among students.
Commitment: ensure consistent attendance and dedication from student participants.

Administration and regulation
School policies: check the school's/college's policies regarding extracurricular activities.
Support: from your senior management team.
Safety regulations: ensure everything meets safety standards.

Performance rights
Licensing: secure rights to perform the chosen play and adhere strictly to licensing agreements.

It is perhaps no coincidence that the constraints outweigh the positives, which is why we have to devise strategies to overcome them.

Time
Create a rehearsal schedule that accommodates academic commitments.
Utilize available spaces creatively, including after-school hours and weekends.
Run this by your colleagues (proposed copy in the staffroom) so that potential clashes/concerns can be flagged.

Budget management
Prioritize expenses, seek funding and donations.
Organize fundraising events and seek sponsorships.

Maximizing resources
Utilize students' talents and encourage cross-curricular collaboration.
Borrow or make costumes and props to reduce costs.
Sell the idea of the show during drama, and other, lessons.
Offer workshops and training sessions to enhance students' skills.
Encourage peer mentoring and leadership roles among students.

Community engagement
Involve parents and community members to support various aspects of production.
Build partnerships with local theatres and arts organizations for additional resources and expertise.

Let's break it down . . .

The value of a school production to the individual student is at the core of my thinking. 'Know your students' applies equally to casting a school play as it does to finding the right script for an exam performance or stimulus for devised work. You may really want to do *Fiddler on the Roof*, but if your students' skill set cries out for *Oliver!*, you do *Oliver!* You may have a burning desire to stage *Annie*, but if you don't have an Annie, then do something else . . . There's always next year. If it's going to be a musical, you will need to seek the support of a strong musical team. Do the students have the vocal range and maturity for the chosen piece? Can the school orchestrate it if needed? What would be their time frame? With a musical, the chances are you will need a choreographer and students who can either dance or be taught to dance.

Consider the school's culture and values.

Before seeking performing rights, it's crucial to consult with key stakeholders including principals, senior management, governors, school board officials, academy trustees, parents, other teachers and students. Obtain guidance from the head/principal and board regarding acceptable content, such as replacing profanity or avoiding 'adult' themes. Seek input from parents and governing bodies before trying to license a show. Generate a list of potential options and discuss them with all relevant parties involved in the school's administration. If uncertain about a show's suitability, provide parents with access to the script for review. While some may have concerns about certain content, it's important to remember that challenging themes are integral to theatre, it's a part of what we do; but ensure the support of both students and the school community before going ahead with such shows.

Purists will say the that theatre should challenge and make you question things as you leave. All true and laudable. However, in your first school show, if the audience go home happy and humming the songs, you've succeeded! Aim to *challenge your cast and entertain your audience*. There are many well-known, highly popular shows that can help you do this, but it's important to keep the following key considerations in mind.

Audience appropriateness: ensure the play is suitable for the intended audience in terms of age, cultural sensitivities and community values. If you're new to the area or simply unsure, check with senior and well-established members of staff/governors.

Scripts and rights: assess the availability of material such as the scripts/score/libretto and licensing rights. Then consider if the technical expertise necessary is available.

Originality and creativity: explore both classic and contemporary plays, weighing the benefits of familiarity with the excitement of introducing new and innovative works. I believe that, if possible, we should alternate.

Relevance and engagement: select a play that resonates with the students and the community, and that sparks interest and engagement with the performers and the audience.

Casting opportunities: choose a play that offers diverse roles suited to the talents and abilities of the students auditioning, ensuring that everyone who wants to has a chance to participate and to shine.

Production requirements: assess the logistical requirements of the play, including sets, costumes, props and effects, to ensure they are feasible within your budget, resources and skill set.

Time: can it be done in the available time? You must consider whether the whole thing is possible and manageable within the available rehearsal time, minus holidays and any other lost rehearsal times. (Musicals take longer!)

Themes and messages: reflect on the themes and messages conveyed by the play, considering their relevance and potential impact on students and their community.

For a variety of reasons, some schools take more convincing of the value of a school production. Sometimes we passionate directors have to remind ourselves we are in a school, not a theatre! For this reason, we must be very sure to consider and then highlight the following.

- Skill development and educational value: consider which materials provide the best opportunity for students to develop and showcase their acting, singing, dancing and other performance skills. In order to evaluate a script's suitability, you need to carefully consider the following factors to ensure it is appropriate, engaging and feasible for your school.
- Understand the audience and purpose: ensure the content is suitable for the age group of your performers and audience. If you are looking for educational value, look for scripts that offer educational benefits, whether in the form of moral lessons, historical contexts, or social messages. Choose a script that will captivate and entertain both the performers and the audience.
- Assess the story and themes: ensure the plot is coherent, compelling and has a clear beginning, middle and end. Consider the themes and whether they align with the values and objectives of your school. Look for well-defined conflicts and satisfying resolutions that offer opportunities for dramatic expression.
- Character analysis: check if the script offers a variety of roles – in terms of complexity, gender, age and personality – to ensure inclusivity and provide opportunities for different students to shine.
- Dialogue and language: is the language appropriate and understandable for the performers' age group? Look for natural, engaging and dynamic dialogue that will be interesting for both actors and audience.
- Production considerations: assess whether the script's requirements for sets, props and costumes are feasible within your budget and resources. Consider technical aspects such as lighting, sound effects and special effects, and whether they are manageable within your

capabilities. Make sure the script's length is suitable for the allotted performance time and that the pacing will keep the audience engaged.
- Casting and ensemble balance: ensure the cast size matches the number of students available to participate. Consider scripts that provide opportunities for ensemble work and ensure that all students who want to have meaningful participation. Does the show have specific race requirements? Colourblind casting is one thing, but certain shows (such as *Hairspray*, *Othello* or *Miss Saigon*) have specific racial requirements that must be adhered to, or else it will affect the piece. For instance, casting a white actor as Othello may undermine the racial dynamics the play is built upon.
- Feedback and consultation: seek opinions from other teachers, drama professionals, or experienced students. Consider potential audience reactions and whether the script is likely to be well received.
- Rights and royalties (see Chapter 7): ensure the script is available for performance and that you can obtain the necessary rights. Ensure the same play isn't being produced at any neighbouring schools/colleges currently, or has been recently. Don't forget to factor in the cost of acquiring performance rights and royalties into your budget.
- Personal connection: choose a script that you can be passionate about and excited to direct. Your enthusiasm will be contagious and inspire your students.

There are many different types of show out there. Let's investigate some and consider their individual pros and cons.

The types of material available

Musicals

Classic musicals (e.g. *The Sound of Music, Oklahoma!*)
   Pros: classic musicals are popular and well-loved by audiences, resulting in sell-out shows. They often contain well-known songs that are enjoyable to perform and watch.
   Cons: they can be resource-intensive. In other words, expensive! In addition, they require students with singing, acting and (usually) dancing abilities. They also require a musical director and a choreographer.

Contemporary musicals (e.g. *Wicked, Hamilton* [schools edition], *Seussical.*)
   Pros: they engage students with modern music styles and themes. They tend to attract larger audiences due to current popularity.
   Cons: rights can be expensive and difficult to obtain. They demand significant talent and resources to do justice to the production and meet expectations. They also require a musical director and a choreographer.

Plays

Classic plays encompass works from ancient Greece and Rome, and works by Shakespeare and other renowned classical playwrights. These plays are frequently studied in schools and are often free from copyright and licensing restrictions, making them widely accessible.

However, it is important to verify the copyright status before use.

Pros: rich in literary and historical value. They offer educational opportunities for students to engage with classic literature and often contain well-established staging and performance guides.

Cons: the language and themes might be challenging for younger students, and sometimes require extensive memorization and understanding of complex dialogue.

Contemporary plays are modern works that address current issues, societal norms and contemporary themes, whilst covering a range of styles and themes. Examples include *Almost, Maine; Top Girls; DNA; The Curious Incident of The Dog in the Nighttime.*

Pros: they are often more relatable to modern audiences and students, and more likely to address contemporary issues and themes.

Cons: contemporary plays may still require significant effort to understand and perform effectively. In addition, availability and performance rights can sometimes be an issue.

Comedies are intended to entertain and amuse. They feature humour, witty dialogue and amusing situations. Examples include *Charley's Aunt, Noises Off, Blithe Spirit.*

Pros: they are fun and entertaining, often light-hearted and enjoyable experience for both performers and the audience. They are likely to attract a larger audience due to their entertaining nature.

Cons: they often require a great deal of time and effort for rehearsals, costumes and set design. Comedy can be subjective and harder to execute effectively, potentially leading to mixed audience reactions. Comedy often carries a risk of stereotyping and limits student exposure to diverse characters.

Historical plays depict events, people and periods from history. They are often epic in scale and ambition. Examples include *Boudica, Julius Caesar, Our Country's Good.*

Pros: they teach students about historical events and figures, making history more engaging and memorable. They promote understanding of different eras and cultures.

Cons: they require time for research and creating period-appropriate sets and costumes.

It can be challenging to accurately portray historical events. They may not attract as wide an audience as other genres. While not a negative, you need to be aware that you may be dealing with sensitive or controversial historical topics.

Experimental or avant-garde plays push the boundaries of traditional theatre with unconventional storytelling techniques, non-linear narratives, and abstract themes offering unique and challenging opportunities for exploration of performance and staging. Consider the maturity of your students. Examples include *The Bald Soprano, Waiting for Godot, Oh! What a Lovely War.*

Pros: they encourage students to think outside the box and explore innovative ideas.

They enhance improvisation and adaptability, and foster a deeper understanding of different artistic expressions and styles. They keep students actively engaged and invested in the creative process, often breaking conventions.

Cons: they can be difficult to execute and understand, requiring advanced skills. They may need unique props, sets and costumes, increasing costs and preparation time. (However, you may have a very minimalist vision). There is always a risk of confusing or alienating the audience, potentially leading to mixed reactions. Not all students may be prepared or interested in such unconventional styles, leading to varied commitment levels.

Children's plays are often tailored specifically for young audiences, feature simple plots, colourful characters, and interactive elements. Examples include *A Midsummer Night's Dream – A Musical for Schools, Archie Dobson's War, Charlotte's Web, James and the Giant Peach* or *Seussical.*

Pros: as long as the material is age appropriate, it captures the interest and enthusiasm of younger students, fostering a love for theatre early on. The narratives are simple and easy for younger students to understand, memorize and perform. You are likely to attract support and attendance from parents and families, strengthening the school community. They always create a joyful and light-hearted experience for both participants and the audience.

Cons: Always remember the age appropriateness and consider that the material may not provide enough complexity or depth for older or more advanced students.

Some materials may limit opportunities for students to explore a wider range of characters and themes. There is also a risk of repeating well-known children's stories, potentially leading to a lack of variety and excitement. They primarily appeal to younger audiences, which might limit broader community interest.

One-act plays are shorter plays with a single act, often performed as part of a series or festival. Often intimate studio performances designed for a smaller audience. Examples include *The Lottery, Angry Pigs, The Zoo* and, for younger students, *The Three Little Pigs*. See also fairy tales and folklore tales which have been adapted for stage.

Pros: the shorter duration makes them easier to rehearse and perform. There are also lower production costs (and often smaller cast). They are ideal for festivals or competitions and good for showcasing a variety of talent in a single event.

Cons: limited time to develop complex characters and plots. May not draw as large an audience as full-length plays or musicals.

Adaptations are plays adapted from novels, short stories, films or other sources, and reimagined for the stage (e.g. *Lord of The Flies, Of Mice and Men*). For younger students, plays such as *The Lion King Kids* or *Peter Pan Jr* provide opportunities to engage with familiar stories and characters.

Pros: students and audiences are often familiar with the story, which lends an understanding born of prior plot and character knowledge. They enhance students' literary appreciation and understanding of the source material. They often offer complex characters and rich narratives, providing challenging roles for students. Cross-curricular learning fosters great engagement between the performing arts and literature. They attract audiences familiar with the novel, potentially increasing attendance and interest.

Cons: they may require significant time and resources to create sets, costumes and props that align with the novel's setting. Audiences and performers may have high expectations based on their familiarity with the novel, leading to potential disappointment. Novels often have intricate plots and numerous characters, which can be challenging to translate effectively onto the stage. The balancing of faithfulness to the novel with practical stage adaptation can be difficult, which has been known to lead to the storytelling being compromised.

Cultural or diversity plays are performances celebrating the traditions, customs or perspectives of various cultures or minority groups, promoting inclusivity and understanding. Check with the school's policies, but a list could include: *True Brits, The Usual Auntijies, Barber Shop Chronicles, Blood, In The Heights*. Engaging and age-appropriate material for younger students includes *Androcles and The Lion, The Rainbow Fish, Anansi The Spider*.

Pros: such material promotes awareness and understanding of different cultures and diverse perspectives. They encourage inclusivity and representation, giving voice to marginalized communities; they also enhance students' empathy, cultural sensitivity and ability to portray diverse characters authentically. They can strengthen community ties by celebrating cultural diversity and potentially attracting a diverse audience. They address contemporary social issues, making the performance timely and meaningful; helping students develop a deeper understanding of their own cultural identities and those of others.

Cons: they require careful handling of cultural themes to avoid stereotypes, misrepresentation or cultural appropriation; demanding extensive research to ensure accuracy and respect for the culture being portrayed. There is always the possibility that it may spark controversy or backlash if not executed thoughtfully, particularly around sensitive topics. There are also casting challenges around ensuring diverse and appropriate casting; particularly where the school community is less diverse. There is a risk of mixed reactions from the audience, as cultural plays can challenge preconceptions and comfort zones; but that is what great theatre is about.

Forum theatre is a kind of interactive performance, where the audience becomes actively involved to offer suggestions, alternative actions and solutions to conflicts. This works well with Theatre in Education (TIE) projects. It is for older students only, however, and is usually used to address and explore real-life issues within a theatrical context. Themes could include bullying, peer pressure, drugs and prejudices.

Pros: they engage students in active participation, fostering deeper understanding and empathy towards social issues, encouraging them to analyse and problem-solve, as they explore different perspectives and solutions to complex problems. It is very empowering, giving students a voice for their opinions and to enact change. It stimulates dialogue and discussion within the school community, fostering a culture of open communication and collaboration. It is a very versatile/adaptable format which allows for the exploration of a wide range of social issues and topics relevant to students' lives.

Cons: as you and your cast will be the main source of the material, you will require extra time to research, workshop and create the piece. You will be dealing with sensitive or controversial topics which require careful handling. Digging into real-life issues can be emotionally taxing for both performers and audience members, requiring appropriate support mechanisms. Balancing the theatrical elements with the educational goals of forum theatre requires careful planning and execution, and it may simply not be what you want as a whole-school play. However, it could be appropriate for a smaller TIE-based studio audience.

Forum brings with it more than the usual logistical challenges, like coordinating rehearsals and managing the interactive nature of forum theatre. In addition, encouraging audience members to actively engage in the performance may be challenging, especially if they are hesitant or unfamiliar with forum theatre conventions.

Variety shows and revues

Talent shows: to me, a talent show is not a school play; I include it as an alternative when time is of the essence or as another possibility for the department's repertoire. A school talent show typically involves students showcasing their diverse talents; such as singing, dancing, playing musical instruments, comedy acts, or even performing selected scenes from plays. It is, in my opinion, a non-competitive event focused on celebrating students' skills and creativity. The format can vary, with individual or group performances, and may include emcees or hosts to guide the event.

Pros: they highlight a wide range of student talents and have low preparation requirements compared to scripted shows.

Cons: they can be less cohesive and professionally polished, and quality and interest may vary significantly between acts.

Revues are productions that showcase a selection of songs, scenes or dances from various musicals, rather than performing a single, full-length musical. They are often organized around a specific theme, such as Broadway hits, Disney classics, or past productions.

Pros: they are simple and flexible. Unlike a traditional musical, it doesn't follow a single storyline; instead, it's a series of standalone performances.

Cons: some students will feel less connected without a full story/plot. A revue also often needs varied costumes, props and set changes for different numbers, which can increase the complexity and cost.

Skits and sketches typically involve short comedy or dramatic scenes. These often revolve around a specific theme or concept and may include elements of improvisation or scripted dialogue. They are designed to entertain the audience and showcase the talents and creativity of the students involved.

Pros: they are flexible and often student-written, and are good for addressing current school or community issues humorously.

Cons: they often lack the depth of longer performances, requiring creativity and strong comedic timing.

Film and multimedia shows

These can offer a dynamic and innovative alternative to a traditional school play. It could take the place of a traditional production in the following ways. Instead of live performances on stage, students could act out scenes that are recorded and edited into a cohesive film. This allows for more precise control over performances and multiple takes to achieve the desired outcome. The incorporation of multimedia can involve combinations of live-action footage, animation, music, sound effects and visual effects to create a visually stunning and immersive experience for the audience.

Pros: films can be screened at various locations and times, providing more flexibility for scheduling and accommodating larger audiences. They can also be easily shared online for broader accessibility. Students can learn valuable skills in video production, editing, sound design and graphic design through the process of creating a film or multimedia show. A well-produced film or multimedia show can captivate audiences and evoke powerful emotions, similar to a live theatrical performance. It can still convey the same level of storytelling and artistic expression as a traditional play, but in a different format. There are many opportunities to incorporate new technologies such as AI, which students can explore effortlessly.

Cons: they require access to filmmaking equipment, software and technical expertise. Production and editing processes can be lengthy, requiring significant time commitments from students and teachers. Technical issues such as filming, editing, and sound quality may arise, requiring troubleshooting and problem-solving.

Whilst exciting and challenging, it does lack the immediate interaction and energy of live theatre, potentially diminishing the sense of connection between the performers and the audience.

Pantomime

'Panto', for short, is a form of musical comedy stage production traditionally performed during the Christmas and New Year season (so consider the school calendar). Originating in the United Kingdom, pantomime blends elements of slapstick comedy, fairy tale, folklore and audience participation, making it a popular form of family entertainment.

Pantomimes typically retell well-known stories such as *Cinderella, Aladdin, Jack and the Beanstalk,* and *Snow White.* Schools often write their own pantos, which are broadly based on well-known tales. While this is great fun, it is also very time-consuming. Costumes and sets should be bright and colourful, creating a fantastical magical world with wonderful opportunities for special effects.

Pros: pantos are great fun and can bring together families and the school community, particularly during the festive season. They are interactive, engaging and inclusive. There are roles for all, with large and varied casts offering villains, heroes, animals and more! There is a great deal of creative freedom, with opportunities for students to contribute creatively in many ways.

Cons: the very things that make panto so appealing can also give you the biggest headaches; for example, they require elaborate sets, costumes and possibly special effects, which can be resource-intensive. They also need skilled direction/choreography for the dance and musical elements.

The tradition of gender-swapping roles might need sensitive handling to ensure inclusivity and avoid potential discomfort. Some of those traditional elements might need adaptation to be culturally appropriate and inclusive. Then there's audience participation! Not all audience members may be comfortable with interactive elements, which can affect the atmosphere if not managed well.

Opera

A dramatic work combining a text (libretto) and a musical score, typically featuring elaborate staging and strong emphasis on vocal performance. It should be aimed at older students really, and only attempted with strong singers and a very competent musical director/department.

Pros: students develop singing techniques, musicality and an understanding of opera as a musical genre. They gain an appreciation for classical music and opera, which are important art forms, exposing them to different historical periods, cultures and artistic expressions.

Producing an opera can enhance the school's reputation and prestige within the community. It engages parents and the community, which can lead to increased support and interest in the school's arts programmes.

Cons: there are high costs associated with producing an opera; including hiring vocal coaches, renting or purchasing costumes, and potentially hiring musicians. An opera requires significant rehearsal/training time, which can be challenging to balance with academic commitments. They are often more technically demanding than regular plays, both vocally and musically. The foreign languages used in many operas can also be a barrier for students and audiences who are not familiar with them.

Operas typically have fewer roles than regular plays, which might limit the number of students who can participate. They will require students with a certain level of vocal ability, potentially excluding those who are less musically inclined.

The demanding nature of opera can put significant pressure on students, leading to stress and performance anxiety. The precision required in opera singing and performance can lead to a perfectionist attitude, which will not be suitable for all students or staff.

If you really fancy doing an opera, choose a shorter, more manageable one (or selected scenes from a longer one), rather than a full-length production. Consider adapting the opera to suit the students' abilities and the school's resources. This can include translating the text into the students' native language and finding ways to involve as many students as possible, perhaps through a chorus or non-singing roles. You could consider approaching local opera companies or university music departments, for support and collaboration.

The nativity

A school nativity play is a cherished, traditional theatrical production depicting the birth of Jesus and performed as close to Christmas as the school term allows. Often the highlight of a school's festive activities, it is usually associated with younger students in primary/elementary school. However, I once did a secondary/high school version using sections from *The Nativity* from Tony Harrison's *The Mysteries* (see Chapter 24).

Pros: a school nativity play involves students in an important cultural and religious story, engaging parents and the wider community, fostering a sense of unity. It enhances the school spirit and creates lasting memories for students and their families. The nativity play offers great opportunities for students to express themselves creatively through acting, singing and dancing. Often a great confidence-building first experience of the theatre for younger students.

Cons: they require significant time for rehearsals, which can be challenging to fit into the pre-Christmas school schedule.

As the nativity play is based on a Christian story, it might not be for all families, and those from different religious or non-religious backgrounds potentially may feel excluded. Some students might feel uncomfortable with the religious content.

Try to avoid stereotyping and typecasting. Know your students and the community.

In the following chapter, 'What's out there?' I present a list of numerous resources, although it is not an exhaustive compilation of all the available material.

One more thing . . .

I have found that organizing a major production every other year, alternating with one or two smaller studio performances, is an effective approach. Some schools, with larger faculties and more staff to share the workload, may manage a large production annually alongside smaller performances. However, keep in mind that many students tend to want to participate in everything, which can become overwhelming and potentially impact their studies.

4

What's out there?

School shows are like a box of chocolates. The endless options are mouthwatering, but if you choose the wrong one for your school, you may end up with a not-so-funny taste in your mouth. Musicals, dramas, comedies, tragedies; there's something for every taste, talent and attention span. The sheer number of shows out there can baffle even the most seasoned teacher, but fear not! This chapter is here to help you navigate the theatrical chocolate box, and find that perfect show for you and your school. However, each suggestion should be thoroughly researched. Look online (YouTube) at other schools' productions or professional shows and ask yourself: could I direct that? Do I currently have the students? Do we have the right venue/stage? If it's a musical, speak to your musical director (MD); are they confident enough to take it on?

If this is your first production, start with something you are familiar with; something straightforward that will ensure success and build student confidence. It's about building a tradition of great productions.

For those with more experience and a strong, capable team, the possibilities are endless. I invite you to peruse the following list of both plays and musicals.

The school play is beyond mere entertainment, it should also serve as a showcase for the school's facilities and the diverse talents of its students. It goes beyond exam results, inviting everyone to witness the magic unfold under the spotlight. While our minds may conjure up grand musicals on the proscenium arch stage, there's much more out there. Let's have a look.

Please note that the following suggestions are only a guide. Scripts may differ, and some shows may have multiple licensing holders, where I show one. The remainder of this chapter lists 100 musical and 100 plays, including ten by Shakespeare.

Musicals

9 to 5
Cast: medium (10–20 principal roles, plus ensemble)
Ages: older teens
Licence: Music Theatre International (MTI)

A Gentleman's Guide to Love and Murder
Cast: medium (10–20 principal roles, plus ensemble)
Ages: older teens
Licence: Concord Theatricals

A Year with Frog and Toad
Cast: small to medium (10–15 principal roles)
Ages: all ages
Licence: MTI

Aida (school edition)
Cast: medium (10–20 principal roles, plus ensemble)
Ages: older teens
Licence: MTI

Alice in Wonderland (Disney's)
Cast: medium (10–20 principal roles, plus ensemble)
Ages: all ages
Licence: MTI

Aladdin (Disney's)
Cast: medium to large (20+ principal roles, plus ensemble)
Ages: all ages
Licence: MTI

Annie
Cast: medium to large (10–20+ principal roles, plus ensemble)
Ages: all ages
Licence: MTI
MTI also has a 60-minute *Annie Jr* and a 30-minute *Annie Kids*

Annie Get Your Gun
Cast: medium (10–20 principal roles, plus ensemble)
Ages: all ages
Licence: Concord Theatricals

Anything Goes
Cast: medium to large (20+ principal roles, plus ensemble)
Ages: older teens
Licence: Concord Theatricals

Big Fish
Cast: medium (10–20 principal roles, plus ensemble)
Ages: all ages
Licence: Theatrical Rights Worldwide (TRW)

Big River
Cast: medium (10–20 principal roles, plus ensemble)
Ages: all ages
Licence: Concord Theatricals

Be More Chill
Cast: medium (10–20 principal roles, plus ensemble)
Ages: older teens
Licence: Concord Theatricals

Beauty and the Beast
Cast: medium to large (20+ principal roles, plus ensemble)
Ages: all ages
Licence: MTI; very strict licensing

Band Geeks
Cast: medium (10–20 principal roles, plus ensemble)
Ages: all ages
Licence: Concord Theatricals

Blood Brothers
Cast: small (8 roles; multi-role, flexible)
Ages: older teens
Licence: Concord Theatricals

Bring It On
Cast: medium (12 roles, plus ensemble)
Ages: 13+
Licence: MTI

Bubble Boy
Cast: medium (10–20 principal roles, plus ensemble)
Ages: older teens
Licence: MTI

Carrie The Musical
Cast: medium (8 female, 6 male, plus ensemble)
Ages: older teens
Licence: Concord Theatricals

Catch Me If You Can
Cast: medium to large (20+ principal roles, plus ensemble)
Ages: older teens
Licence: MTI

Children of Eden
Cast: medium to large (20+ principal roles, plus ensemble)
Ages: all ages
Licence: MTI

Chitty Chitty Bang Bang
Cast: medium to large (20+ principal roles, plus ensemble)
Ages: all ages
Licence: MTI

Cinderella (**Rodgers and Hammerstein**)
Cast: medium to large (20+ principal roles, plus ensemble)
Ages: all ages
Licence: Concord Theatricals

Cry-Baby
Cast: medium (10–20 principal roles, plus ensemble)
Ages: older teens
Licence: MTI

Dear Edwina
Cast: medium (10–20 principal roles, plus ensemble)
Ages: all ages
Licence: MTI

Disaster!
Cast: medium (10–20 principal roles, plus ensemble)
Ages: older teens
Licence: MTI

Dream Girls
Cast: small to medium (4 female, 4 male, plus ensemble)
Ages: older students
Licence: Concord Theatricals

Emma! A Pop Musical
Cast: medium (10–20 principal roles, plus ensemble)
Ages: all ages
Licence: Broadway Licensing

Fame
Cast: medium to large (20+ principal roles, plus ensemble)
Ages: older teens
Licence: Concord Theatricals

Firebringer
Cast: small to medium (10–15 principal roles)
Ages: older teens
Licence: Starkid Productions

Fiddler on the Roof
Cast: medium to large (20+ principal roles, plus ensemble)
Ages: older teens
Licence: MTI. Restrictions may apply. Processing time for applications may exceed normal wait times. Strict choreographic stipulations.

Footloose
Cast: medium to large (20+ principal roles, plus ensemble)
Ages: older teens
Licence: Concord Theatricals

Freaky Friday (Disney's)
Cast: medium (10–20 principal roles, plus ensemble)
Ages: all ages
Licence: MTI

Godspell
Cast: medium (10–20 principal roles, plus ensemble)
Ages: older teens
Licence: MTI

Ghost the Musical
Cast: medium (10–20 principal roles, plus ensemble)
Ages: older teens
Licence: TRW

Grease
Cast: medium (10–20 principal roles, plus ensemble)
Ages: older teens
Licence: Concord Theatricals. A high royalty title!

Guys and Dolls
Cast: medium (10–20 principal roles, plus ensemble)
Ages: all ages
Licence: MTI

Hairspray
Cast: medium to large (20+ principal roles, plus ensemble)
Ages: all ages
Licence: MTI

Heathers (The teen edition)
Cast: 10F 14M plus ensemble
Ages: older teens
Licence: Concord Theatricals

High School Musical
Cast: medium to large (20+ principal roles, plus ensemble)
Ages: all ages
Licence: MTI

How to Succeed in Business Without Really Trying
Cast: medium (10–20 principal roles, plus ensemble)
Ages: older teens
Licence: MTI

Honk!
Cast: medium (10–20 principal roles, plus ensemble)
Ages: all ages
Licence: MTI

Into the Woods
Cast: medium (10–20 principal roles, plus ensemble)
Ages: all ages
Licence: MTI

James and the Giant Peach
Cast: medium (10–20 principal roles, plus ensemble)
Ages: all ages
Licence: MTI

Jekyll and Hyde
Cast: medium (10–20 principal roles, plus ensemble)
Ages: older teens
Licence: MTI

Joseph and the Amazing Technicolor Dreamcoat
Cast: medium to large (20+ principal roles, plus ensemble)
Ages: all ages
Licence: Concord Theatricals

Kiss Me, Kate
Cast: medium (10–20 principal roles, plus ensemble)
Ages: older teens
Licence: Concord Theatricals

Legally Blonde
Cast: medium to large (20+ principal roles, plus ensemble)
Ages: older teens
Licence: MTI

Les Misérables (school edition)
Cast: medium to large (20+ principal roles, plus ensemble)
Ages: older teens
Licence: MTI

Little Shop of Horrors
Cast: small to medium (10–15 principal roles, plus ensemble)
Ages: older teens
Licence: MTI restrictions may apply!

Mamma Mia!
Cast: medium to large (20+ principal roles, plus ensemble)
Ages: older teens
Licence: MTI

Mary Poppins
Cast: medium to large (20+ principal roles, plus ensemble)
Ages: all ages
Licence: MTI

Matilda
Cast: medium to large (20+ principal roles, plus ensemble)
Ages: all ages
Licence: MTI

Mean Girls (school version)
Cast: small (9 principal roles, plus ensemble)
Ages: older teens
Licence: MTI

My Fair Lady
Cast: medium (10–20 principal roles, plus ensemble)
Ages: all ages
Licence: Concord Theatricals

Newsies
Cast: medium to large (20+ principal roles, plus ensemble)
Ages: all ages
Licence: MTI

Oklahoma!
Cast: medium (10–20 principal roles, plus ensemble)
Ages: all ages
Licence: Concord Theatricals

On the Town
Cast: medium to large (20+ principal roles, plus ensemble)
Ages: older teens
Licence: Concord Theatricals

Oliver!
Cast: medium to large (17 principal roles, plus ensemble)
Ages: older teens
Licence: MTI

Our Day Out (revised musical play version)
Cast: large flexible
Ages: older teens
Licence: Concord Theatricals

Pippin
Cast: medium (10–20 principal roles, plus ensemble)
Ages: older teens
Licence: MTI

Peter Pan
Cast: medium to large (20+ principal roles, plus ensemble)
Ages: all ages (there is also a junior version) MTI
Licence: Concord Theatricals. The original 1904 play by J. M. Barrie remains under the special royalty rights of Great Ormond Street Hospital (GOSH) in the UK.

Rock of Ages (high school edition)
Cast: medium to large (20+ principal roles, plus ensemble)
Ages: older teens
Licence: Concord Theatricals

Ruthless
Cast: small (7 all-female leads; 1 male voice)
Ages: older teens
Licence: Concord Theatricals

Saturday Night Fever
Cast: large (6 Female, 7 Male plus 1, plus ensemble)
Ages: older teens
Licence: Broadway Licensing Global

Sister Act
Cast: medium to large (20+ principal roles, plus ensemble)
Ages: older teens
Licence: MTI

School of Rock
Cast: medium (10–20 principal roles, plus ensemble)
Ages: all ages
Licence: Concord Theatricals

Shrek The Musical
Cast: small (7 principal roles, plus ensemble)
Ages: 11+
Licence: MTI

Singin' in the Rain
Cast: medium to large (20+ principal roles, plus ensemble)
Ages: all ages
Licence: Concord Theatricals

Songs for a New World
Cast: small (4–8 principal roles)
Ages: older teens
Licence: MTI

Sweeney Todd (school edition)
Cast: medium (10–20 principal roles, plus ensemble)
Ages: older teens
Licence: MTI

Seussical
Cast: medium (10–20 principal roles, plus ensemble)
Ages: all ages
Licence: MTI

The 25th Annual Putnam County Spelling Bee
Cast: small (10–12 principal roles)
Ages: older teens
Licence: MTI

The Addams Family
Cast: medium (10–20 principal roles, plus ensemble)
Ages: all ages
Licence: TRW

The Baker's Wife
Cast: medium (10–20 principal roles, plus ensemble)
Ages: older teens
Licence: Concord Theatricals

The Boyfriend
Cast: medium (10 principal roles, plus ensemble)
Ages: teenage plus
Licence: MTI

The Drowsy Chaperone
Cast: medium (10–20 principal roles, plus ensemble)
Ages: older teens
Licence: MTI

The Fantasticks
Cast: small (8 principal roles)
Ages: older teens
Licence: MTI

The Gruffalo Play by Julia Donaldson
Cast: 5 roles (narrator)
Ages: 5+
Licence: Noble Beast Theatricals manages the stage adaptation rights in some regions, or contact Macmillan Children's Books, the publisher, for guidance.

The Jungle Book (Disney's)
Cast: medium (10–20 principal roles, plus ensemble)
Ages: all ages
Licence: MTI

The King and I
Cast: medium (13+ principal roles, plus ensemble)
Ages: older teens
Licence: Concord Theatricals (Rodgers and Hammerstein)

The Lightning Thief: The Percy Jackson Musical
Cast: medium (10–20 principal roles, plus ensemble)
Ages: all ages
Licence: Concord Theatricals

The Lion King Jr.
Cast: medium (17 principal roles, plus ensemble)
Ages: all ages
Licence: MTI

The Little Mermaid
Cast: medium to large (20+ principal roles, plus ensemble)
Ages: all ages
Licence: MTI

The Nativity by Niki Davies
Cast: large (25+ principal roles)
Ages: 4+
Licence: an annual performance licence is required from Out of the Ark Music.

Meet Me in St. Louis
Cast: medium (12 principal roles)
Ages: older teens
Licence: Concord Theatricals

The Music Man
Cast: large (13+ principal roles, plus large ensemble)
Ages: 11+
Licence: MTI

The Mystery of Edwin Drood
Cast: medium (10–20 principal roles)
Ages: older teens
Licence: Concord Theatricals

The Pajama Game
Cast: medium (10–20 principal roles, plus ensemble)
Ages: older teens
Licence: Concord Theatricals

The Pirates of Penzance
Cast: medium (10–20 principal roles, plus ensemble)
Ages: all ages
Licence: Concord Theatricals/public domain (for original text)

The Secret Diary Of Adrian Mole Aged 13¾ The Musical
Cast: small (6+, flexible)
Ages: older teens
Licence: Concord Theatricals

The Secret Garden
Cast: medium (10–20 principal roles, plus ensemble)
Ages: all ages
Licence: Concord Theatricals

The Sound of Music
Cast: medium (10–20 principal roles, plus ensemble)
Ages: all ages
Licence: Concord Theatricals

The Theory of Relativity
Cast: small to medium (10–15 principal roles)
Ages: older teens
Licence: MTI

The Wiz
Cast: medium to large (20+ principal roles, plus ensemble)
Ages: all ages
Licence: Concord Theatricals

Thoroughly Modern Millie
Cast: medium to large (20+ principal roles, plus ensemble)
Ages: older teens
Licence: MTI

Tuck Everlasting
Cast: medium (10–20 principal roles, plus ensemble)
Ages: all ages
Licence: Concord Theatricals

West Side Story
Cast: medium (10 principal roles, plus large ensemble)
Ages: older teens
Licence: MTI

Whistle Down The Wind
Cast: medium (14 principal roles, plus ensemble)
Ages: older teens
Licence: Josef Weinberger, MTI

You're a Good Man, Charlie Brown
Cast: small (6–10 principal roles)
Ages: all ages
Licence: Concord Theatricals

Zombie Prom
Cast: medium (10–20 principal roles, plus ensemble)
Ages: older teens
Licence: Concord Theatricals

Plays

A Christmas Carol **by Charles Dickens**
Adapted by various playwrights
Genre: drama/fantasy
Cast: large (20+ roles; flexible and easy to mix)
Ages: all ages
Licence: public domain. However, there are numerous adaptations and stage versions, each with their own rights holders.

A Piece of My Heart **by Shirley Lauro**
Genre: drama/history
Cast: small to medium (8–12 roles)
Ages: older teens
Licence: Samuel French

A Raisin in the Sun **by Lorraine Hansberry**
Genre: drama
Cast: medium (10–15 roles)
Ages: older teens
Licence: Concord Theatricals

Abigail's Party **by Mike Leigh**
Genre: comedy/satire
Cast: small
Ages: older teens
Licence: Concord Theatricals

Alice in Wonderland **by Lewis Carroll (adapted by A. C. Martens)**
Genre: children's theatre adaptation
Cast: large (30+), either gender/doubling possible
Ages: all ages
Licence: The Dramatic Publishing Company

All My Sons **by Arthur Miller**
Genre: Drama
Cast: medium (10–15 roles)
Ages: older teens
Licence: Dramatists Play Service

Anne of Green Gables **by L. M. Montgomery**
Adapted by Joseph Robinette
Genre: drama/family
Cast: medium (10–20 roles)
Ages: all ages
Licence: Dramatic Publishing

Antigone by Sophocles, various adaptations
Genre: tragedy
Cast: medium to large (15–20 roles)
Ages: older teens
Licence: various (public domain for original text)

Arsenic and Old Lace by Joseph Kesselring
Genre: comedy/farce
Cast: medium (10–15 roles)
Ages: all ages
Licence: Concord Theatricals

Blithe Spirit by Noël Coward
Genre: comedy/fantasy
Cast: small to medium (8–12 roles)
Ages: older teens
Licence: Concord Theatricals

Blue Remembered Hills by Dennis Potter
Genre: drama
Cast: small (5 male, 2 female roles)
Ages: older teens
Licence: Samuel French

Brighton Beach Memoirs by Neil Simon
Genre: comedy/drama
Cast: small to medium (8–10 roles)
Ages: older teens
Licence: Concord Theatricals

Big Fish by John August
Based on the novel by Daniel Wallace
Genre: drama
Cast: medium (10–20 principal roles, plus ensemble)
Ages: all ages
Licence: TRW

Charley's Aunt by Brandon Thomas
Genre: comedy
Cast: medium (10+ roles)
Ages: older teens
Licence: Concord Theatricals

Charlotte's Web by E. B. White
Adapted by Joseph Robinette

Genre: children's drama
Cast: medium (12 roles, versatile casting)
Ages: younger children and audiences
Licence: Dramatic Publishing (DPC)

Cider With Rosie **by Laurie Lee**
Adapted by Nick Darke
Genre: drama
Cast: medium to large (from 4 female, 5 male to 37, versatile casting)
Ages: teens
Licence: ICM London (Heinemann)

Cluedo **by Sandy Rustin**
Based on the screenplay by Jonathan Lynn
Genre: comedy
Cast: versatile (minimum 5 female, 5 male; up to 20 performers possible)
Ages: teens
Licence: Broadway Licensing Global

Daisy Pulls It Off **by Denise Deegan**
Genre: comedy
Cast: large, mainly female cast
Ages: teens
Licence: Concord Theatricals

Dr Faustus **by Christopher Marlowe**
Genre: classical
Cast: medium (8–12, flexible)
Ages: older teens
Licence: generally in the public domain. However, there may be different rules for translations, adaptations, or specific editions.

Death of a Salesman **by Arthur Miller**
Genre: drama
Cast: medium (10–15 roles)
Ages: older teens
Licence: Dramatists Play Service

Ernie's Incredible Illucinations **by Alan Ayckbourn**
Genre: comedy
Cast: large (22, plus extras)
Ages: 11+
Licence: Samuel French

Harvey by Mary Chase
Genre: comedy
Cast: medium (12–15 roles)
Ages: all ages
Licence: Dramatists Play Service

Middletown by Will Eno
Genre: comedy
Cast: medium (6 female, 6 male)
Ages: older teens
Licence: Concord Theatricals

Peter and the Starcatcher by Rick Elice
Based on the novel by Dave Barry and Ridley Pearson
Genre: drama/comedy
Cast: medium (10–20 roles)
Ages: all ages
Licence: MTI

Puffs, or: Seven Increasingly Eventful Years at a Certain School of Magic and Magic by Matt Cox
Genre: drama/comedy
Cast: 11 (any gender [mature])
Ages: teens
Licence: Concord Theatricals. You can licence either a one-act or two-act version.

Pygmalion by George Bernard Shaw
Genre: comedy
Cast: medium 12+
Ages: older teens
Licence: public domain, but check various versions

Radium Girls by D. W. Gregory
Genre: drama/history
Cast: medium (10–20 roles)
Ages: older teens
Licence: Dramatic Publishing

Rumors by Neil Simon
Genre: comedy/farce
Cast: medium (10–15 roles)
Ages: older teens
Licence: Concord Theatricals

She Kills Monsters by Qui Nguyen
Genre: comedy/fantasy
Cast: medium (10–15 roles)
Ages: older teens
Licence: Concord Theatricals

She Stoops to Conquer by Oliver Goldsmith
Genre: Restoration farce
Cast: small (4 female, 7 male)
Ages: older teens
Licence: public domain

Steel Magnolias by Robert Harling
Genre: drama/comedy
Cast: small (6–8 roles)
Ages: older teens
Licence: Dramatists Play Service

The BFG by David Wood
Adapted from the book by Roald Dahl
Genre: comedy
Cast: small (4 female, 4 male)
Ages: younger students
Licence: Concord Theatricals/Samuel French

The Caucasian Chalk Circle by Bertolt Brecht
Genre: contemporary
Cast: vastly flexible
Ages: older teens
Licence: various versions/check script; Samuel French

The Crucible by Arthur Miller
Genre: drama
Cast: medium to large (20+ roles)
Ages: older teens
Licence: Concord Theatricals/International DPS/Josef Weinberger

The Curious Incident of the Dog in the Night-Time by Simon Stephens
Based on the novel by Mark Haddon
Genre: drama/mystery
Cast: medium (10–15 roles)
Ages: older teens
Licence: Dramatists Play Service

The Diary of Anne Frank by Frances Goodrich and Albert Hackett
Genre: drama/biography
Cast: medium (10–15 roles)
Ages: older teens
Licence: Dramatists Play Service

The House of Bernarda Alba by Federico García Lorca
Genre: classical
Cast: small (10 female)
Ages: older teens
Licence: Concord Theatricals/Samuel French (various translations)

The Importance of Being Earnest by Oscar Wilde
Genre: comedy
Cast: small (8–10 roles)
Ages: all ages
Licence: the original is in the public domain, various adaptations may not be!

The Man Who Came to Dinner by Moss Hart and George S. Kaufman
Genre: comedy
Cast: medium to large (20+ roles)
Ages: all ages
Licence: Dramatists Play Service

The Matchmaker by Thornton Wilder
Genre: comedy
Cast: medium (12–20 roles)
Ages: all ages
Licence: Concord Theatricals

The Miracle Worker by William Gibson
Genre: drama/biography
Cast: medium (10–15 roles)
Ages: all ages
Licence: Concord Theatricals

The Mousetrap by Agatha Christie
Genre: mystery/thriller
Cast: small (8 roles)
Ages: older teens
Licence: Concord Theatricals

The Odd Couple by Neil Simon
Genre: comedy

Cast: small to medium (8–12 roles)
Ages: older teens
Licence: Concord Theatricals

The Outsiders by S. E. Hinton, adapted by Christopher Sergel
Genre: drama
Cast: medium (10–20 roles)
Ages: older teens
Licence: Dramatic Publishing

The Seagull by Anton Chekhov
Genre: realism, tragicomedy
Cast: small, flexible (5 female, 6 male)
Ages: older teens
Licence: Peters Fraser & Dunlop Group

The Skin of Our Teeth by Thornton Wilder
Genre: drama/comedy
Cast: large (20+ roles)
Ages: older teens
Licence: Concord Theatricals

The Tale of Peter Rabbit by Beatrix Potter
Adapted by Lynn Stevens
Genre: drama
Cast: medium (8F 6M)
Ages: younger students
Licence: Concord Theatricals/Samuel French

The Velveteen Rabbit by Margery Williams
Adapted by Philip Grecian. But various playwrights have made adaptations.
Genre: drama/fantasy
Cast: small (2 female, 1 male, plus 8 of any gender)
Ages: 6–10
Licence: DPC Dramatic Publishing

The Women of Lockerbie by Deborah Brevoort
Genre: drama
Cast: medium (10–15 roles)
Ages: older teens
Licence: Dramatists Play Service

Tartuffe by Molière
Genre: drama
Cast: small (8 male, 7 female)

Ages: older teens
Licence: public domain. Beware of some translations though. Samuel French.

To Kill a Mockingbird by **Christopher Sergel**
Based on the novel by Harper Lee
Genre: drama
Cast: medium (10–15 roles)
Ages: older teens
Licence: Dramatic Publishing

Twelve Angry Jurors by **Reginald Rose**
Genre: drama
Cast: small (12 roles)
Ages: older teens
Licence: Dramatic Publishing

Winnie The Pooh by **A. A. Milne**
Adapted by L. Price
Genre: children's theatre (adaptation)
Cast: small (1 male, 1 female, plus 8 gender versatile)
Ages: younger students
Licence: Theatrefolk.com

You Can't Take It With You by **Moss Hart and George S. Kaufman**
Genre: comedy
Cast: medium (12–20 roles)
Ages: all ages
Licence: Concord Theatricals

More challenging works

Many of the following are not merely complex to stage, but can contain challenging themes that are intended for an adult audience.

A Servant to Two Masters by **Carlo Goldini**
Adapted by Lee Hall
Genre: commedia dell'arte
Cast: small (9+ flexible; multi-role)
Ages: older teens
Licence: The Rod Hall Agency (London)

Accidental Death of An Anarchist by **Dario Fo**
Genre: political farce

Cast: small (6 roles)
Ages: older teens
Licence: The Rod Hall Agency (London)

An Inspector Calls by J. B. Priestly
Genre: drama
Cast: small (3 female, 4 male [can be expanded])
Ages: older teens
Licence: The Rod Hall Agency (London)

Blue Stockings by Jessica Swale
Genre: drama
Cast: medium to large (15–20 roles)
Ages: older teens
Licence: Samuel French

Circle Mirror Transformation by Annie Baker
Genre: drama/comedy
Cast: small (5–8 roles)
Ages: older teens
Licence: Dramatists Play Service

Clybourne Park by Bruce Norris
Genre: drama/comedy
Cast: medium (10–15 roles)
Ages: older teens
Licence: Dramatists Play Service

Dancing at Lughnasa by Brian Friel
Genre: drama (memory play)
Cast: small (3 male, 3 female)
Ages: older teens
Licence: Faber & Faber/Samuel French

DNA by Dennis Kelly
Genre: thriller/drama
Cast: small (11, but flexible; any gender)
Ages: older teenagers
Licence: Concord Theatricals/Samuel French

Eurydice by Sarah Ruhl
Genre: drama/fantasy
Cast: small to medium (8–12 roles)
Ages: older teens
Licence: Concord Theatricals

Fear and Misery of the Third Reich by Bertolt Brecht
Genre: historical
Cast: massively flexible (90 any gender; multi-role/cross-casting can reduce this to as few as six)
Ages: older teens
Licence: Samuel French

Girls Like That by Evan Placey
Genre: teen drama
Cast: up to 24 (all-female cast; can be reduced by multi-role)
Ages: older teens
Licence: NHB Nick Hern Books

Journey's End by R. C. Sheriff
Genre: tragedy (war drama)
Cast: 10 (all male)
Ages: teens
Licence: Samuel French

Lord of the Flies by William Golding, adapted by N. Williams
Genre: drama
Cast: small (8–12 males [but has been done with an all-female cast])
Ages: teens
Licence: Faber & Faber (Contact nicola@william-golding.co.uk)

Love and Information by Caryl Churchill
Genre: dramatic comedy
Cast: ensemble cast; opportunities for double casting
Ages: older teenagers
Licence: Concord Theatricals/Samuel French

Metamorphoses by Mary Zimmerman
Genre: drama/fantasy
Cast: medium (10–20 roles)
Ages: older teens
Licence: Concord Theatricals

Metamorphoses by Steven Berkoff
Genre: theatre of the absurd or experimental
Cast: medium (4–6 roles)
Ages: older teens
Licence: Concord Theatricals or the authorized representative listed in the published scripts

Mmmacbeth by Alison Williams
Genre: comedy (adaptation)
Cast: small (5 female, 5 any gender; easily expandable; lots of cast and props!)
Ages: teens
Licence: Theatrefolk.com

Noises off by Michael Frayn
Genre: comedy/farce
Cast: small (4 female, 5 male)
Ages: older teens
Licence: Concord Theatricals/Samuel French

Rabbit Hole by David Lindsay-Abaire
Genre: drama
Cast: small (5–8 roles)
Ages: older teens
Licence: Dramatists Play Service

Red by John Logan
Genre: drama
Cast: small (2 roles)
Ages: older teens
Licence: Dramatists Play Service

Silent Sky by Lauren Gunderson
Genre: drama/biography
Cast: small to medium (8–12 roles)
Ages: older teens
Licence: Dramatists Play Service

The 39 Steps by John Buchan
Adapted by Patrick Barlow
Genre: comedy/thriller
Cast: small (1 female, 1 male, 2 any gender; multi-role)
Ages: older teens
Licence: Concord Theatricals/Samuel French *(Also two abridged versions available)*

The Children's Hour by Lillian Hellman
Genre: drama
Cast: medium (12–15 roles)
Ages: older teens
Licence: Dramatists Play Service

The Effect of Gamma Rays on Man-in-the-Moon Marigolds by Paul Zindel
Genre: drama
Cast: small (5–8 roles)
Ages: older teens
Licence: Dramatists Play Service

The Exonerated by Jessica Blank and Erik Jensen
Genre: drama/docudrama
Cast: small to medium (8–12 roles)
Ages: older teens
Licence: Dramatists Play Service

The Flick by Annie Baker
Genre: drama/comedy
Cast: small (4–6 roles)
Ages: older teens
Licence: Dramatists Play Service

The Glass Menagerie by Tennessee Williams
Genre: drama
Cast: small (5–8 roles)
Ages: older teens
Licence: Dramatists Play Service

The Laramie Project: Ten Years Later by Moisés Kaufman and the Members of the Tectonic Theater Project
Genre: drama/docudrama
Cast: medium (10–15 roles)
Ages: older teens
Licence: Dramatists Play Service

The Moors by Jen Silverman
Genre: drama/comedy
Cast: small to medium (8–12 roles)
Ages: older teens
Licence: Concord Theatricals

The Plot, Like Gravy, Thickens by Billy Wayne St. John
Genre: comedy
Cast: medium (9 female, 5 male)
Ages: older teens
Licence: Concord Theatricals/Smauel French

The Secret in the Wings by Mary Zimmerman
Genre: drama/fantasy

Cast: medium (10–20 roles)
Ages: older teens
Licence: Concord Theatricals

These Shining Lives by Melanie Marnich
Genre: drama/history
Cast: small to medium (8–12 roles)
Ages: older teens
Licence: Dramatists Play Service

Time Stands Still by Donald Margulies
Genre: drama
Cast: small (4–6 roles)
Ages: older teens
Licence: Dramatists Play Service

Waiting for Godot by Samuel Beckett
Genre: absurd
Cast: small (5 roles, all male but could be flexible)
Ages: older teens
Licence: Concord Theatricals/Samuel French

Wit by Margaret Edson
Genre: drama
Cast: small to medium (8–12 roles)
Ages: older teens
Licence: Dramatists Play Service

The Mysteries by Tony Harrison
Genre: chancel drama/pageant, faith-based promenade
Cast: expandable
Ages: older teens
Licence: Concord Theatricals.

There are also a number of excellent websites out there with great materials tailored for school productions; adaptations and short version for younger students are available through companies like Drama Notebook.com or Drama Online National Theatre Collection for Primary Schools.

Shakespeare

A Midsummer Night's Dream
Genre: comedy/fantasy
Cast: large (20+ roles)

Ages: all ages
Licence: public domain

Hamlet
Genre: tragedy
Cast: 22 male, 2 female (flexible with numbers and gender)
Ages: older teens
Licence: public domain

Julius Caesar
Genre: tragedy/historical
Cast: 26 male, 2 female (flexible and easily reduced)
Ages: older teens
Licence: public domain

King Lear
Genre: tragedy
Cast: medium (11 male, 3 female, plus various servants, soldiers, and attendants; flexible)
Ages: teens
Licence: public domain

Macbeth
Genre: tragedy
Cast: large 20 male, 8 female (can be reduced to 5 male, 4 female main characters; flexible)
Ages: teens
Licence: public domain

Much Ado About Nothing
Genre: comedy/romance
Cast: large (20+ roles)
Ages: teens
Licence: public domain

Romeo and Juliet
Genre: tragedy/romance
Cast: large (20+ roles)
Ages: older teens
Licence: public domain

The Tempest
Genre: comedy/romance
Cast: medium (12 male, 2 female; great flexibility with gender and numbers)

Ages: teens
Licence: public domain

The Winter's Tale
Genre: comedy/romantic
Cast: medium (12 male, 6 female; flexible)
Ages: teens
Licence: public domain

Twelfth Night
Genre: comedy/romantic
Cast: medium (10 male, 3 female; plus courtiers and musicians; very versatile)
Ages: teens
Licence: public domain

I list ten plays here but all are possible, depending on venue and students. See Chapter 25, 'A shout-out for Shakespeare!'.

One more thing . . .

I have known teachers to pen plays themselves for their school/students to perform. At my secondary school, our English teacher collaborated with a number of older students and together they created a piece of theatre that was pretty amazing. For me, it's always been a massive ask of any teacher to expect a script/score on top of everything else.

I've considered it when students have devised great material for exams and wanted to widen their audience. I've also known teachers who annually write/adapt material for the school panto and I have great respect for them, but it's not my thing.

Below are some pros and cons associated with writing your own materials.

Pros:

- Tailored: original plays are able to reflect the school's culture, values and student experiences, making them more meaningful.
- Creative expression: teachers can showcase their creativity and passion for storytelling, inspiring students to engage with the arts.
- Student involvement: students can contribute ideas, themes or even collaborate on writing, fostering a sense of ownership and investment in the production.
- Flexibility: scripts can be adapted to suit the talents and interests of the students involved, ensuring a more engaging and relevant performance.

- Skill development: teachers can model the writing process, encouraging students to explore their own writing and performance skills.

Cons:

- Quality concerns: not all teachers may have experience in playwrighting, which could lead to a lower-quality script.
- Time constraints: writing a play can be time-consuming, and teachers may struggle to find the time alongside all the other demands on them.
- Limited perspectives: a single teacher's vision might not encompass diverse viewpoints or experiences, potentially limiting the narrative.
- Risk of overreach: if not done collaboratively, there's a risk that the play may not resonate with the students or the broader school community.

5

Selling it to the boss

My first show was at the request of the head teacher. It went well, so the second was left to me; all I had to do was convince him. I wanted to do a Shakespeare, he wanted another musical. I argued that there was more to theatre than singing and dancing, and that in order to be inclusive, we had to cater for those who could not or did not want to sing, let alone dance. We came away with an agreement to alternate yearly and that the following show would be *Oliver!* This left me to choose a Shakespeare that, in the head's words, 'would not send the audience to sleep or fail to sell tickets'. I feel so strongly about teachers being able to sell Shakespeare to a reluctant audience, cast or boss, that I have written a whole section on it. See Chapter 25, 'A shout-out for Shakespeare!'.

There is a buzz around a school during a production. It builds towards the opening night and even those who are the least involved can sense the energy. It builds towards that moment when drama becomes the very public face of the school, a time when the doors open to welcome the community, inviting them to witness first-hand the talents and capabilities of its students.

In those weeks and months building up to the performance(s), there are many unseen benefits to the school community. A whole-school production fosters a sense of unity, creativity and collaboration among students, teachers and parents.

This chapter aims to highlight the benefits of a school play as learning objectives across the curriculum; effectively demonstrating to senior management, in terms they can appreciate, the cross-curricular educational value of a whole-school production. So let's have one of those lists . . .

Language and literacy

- Enhance reading comprehension: students will analyse and interpret complex texts, such as scripts and plays.
- Develop writing skills: students could write reflective essays, character analyses and critiques.
- Improve oral communication: students should practice clear and expressive speaking, improving diction and projection.

- Expand vocabulary: students will learn new words and phrases specific to the play and dramatic literature.

Social studies and history

- Understand historical context: students could be involved in researching the historical and cultural background of the play's setting and themes.
- Explore societal issues: students will examine the social, political and ethical issues presented in the play.

Art and design

- Develop artistic skills: students will create set designs, costumes and props, applying principles of visual arts.
- Understand art history: students can study the artistic styles and historical periods represented in the play's production design.

Music and performing arts

- Enhance musical abilities: performing students will engage in vocal training and possibly instrumental performance if the play includes musical elements.
- Learn technical skills: some students will operate sound and lighting equipment, enhancing their understanding of technical theatre.

Drama and performance skills

- Character development: students will learn about techniques for creating and sustaining believable characters.
- Improvisation: students will be encouraged to develop spontaneity and creativity through improvisational exercises.
- Script analysis: students will interpret and analyse scripts, understanding narrative structure and character arcs.
- Vocal techniques: students will be introduced to proper breathing, projection and articulation for clear and expressive speech.
- Physical acting: students will use body language, movement and physicality to convey emotions and actions.

Technical theatre skills

- Set design and construction: some students will design and build sets, understanding spatial relationships and construction techniques.
- Costume and make-up: some students will create and apply costumes and make-up, considering historical accuracy and character portrayal.
- Lighting and sound design: some students will design and operate lighting and sound equipment, enhancing the mood and atmosphere of the performance.
- Stage management: some students will manage rehearsals, coordinate backstage activities, and ensure the smooth running of performances.

Mathematics

- Apply mathematical concepts: design students will need to use geometry and measurement in set design and construction.
- Manage budgets: students who choose to work front of house may be involved in calculating costs for production materials and manage a budget for the play. See front of house section.

Science

- Understand acoustics: sound tech students will explore the principles of sound and acoustics in designing effective stage environments.
- Apply physics: students may consider the principles of physics in the construction of sets and special effects.

Physical education

- Enhance physical coordination: students can improve their physical coordination through stage movements and choreography.
- Promote teamwork: students will engage in collaborative activities, fostering teamwork and physical cooperation.

Social and emotional learning (SEL)

- Develop empathy: students will be introduced to and express a range of emotions through character exploration.

- Improve confidence: students may build self-confidence through public performance.
- Enhance collaboration: students will work as part of a team, learning to communicate and collaborate effectively.
- Foster creativity: students will have the opportunity to express their creativity in various aspects of the production process.

Critical thinking and problem-solving

- Analyse and interpret: students will be encouraged to critically analyse characters, themes, and plots.
- Solve problems: students should develop solutions for technical and logistical challenges in production.

Technology

- Utilize digital tools: some students will use digital tools including AI for scriptwriting, designing and creating promotional materials.
- Enhance multimedia skills: students may engage in video editing, digital sound design and other multimedia applications.

Business and marketing

- Learn marketing strategies: students will develop marketing plans to promote the play, including posters, social media campaigns and ticket sales.
- Understand event planning: students will be encouraged to plan and manage events, from rehearsals to performances.

Collaboration and teamwork

- Group dynamics: students will work effectively within a group, understanding the importance of each role in a collaborative project.
- Conflict resolution: students will learn about resolving conflicts and navigating differing opinions in a constructive manner.
- Leadership: students may take on leadership roles, such as directing or leading a team, developing their ability to guide and inspire others.

Also consider parental involvement. When parents become involved in the production process through volunteer opportunities, fundraising or attending performances, it strengthens the partnership between home and school and fosters a sense of pride in the school community.

In addition, the school production is a great celebration of achievement. A whole-school play provides a platform for students to showcase their talents and hard work, celebrating their achievements and creating lasting memories for themselves and their peers.

One more thing . . .

and I admit this one was difficult for me to get my head around! A vital consideration when trying to convince senior management that your production is going to be huge and important and wonderful for all concerned is this: they (the senior management) run a large educational establishment which involves much more than you might imagine and certainly much more than your play. Having said that . . .

6

Selling it to the students

'I want to be in the play but . . .'
  'It's embarrassing!'
  'I don't have time.'
  'My mates will laugh.'
  'No way I'm singing or dancing.'
  'I'd like to help backstage but my dad wants me to be in it.'
  'My parents don't want me wasting my time in a play.'
  'I didn't get a part last year.'
  'I can't sing.'
  'I can't act.'
  'I get nervous.'
  'I'm way too cool.'
  'I'm not that cool.'

To many students, the idea being in the school play is great, it's exciting, it's challenging, a rite of passage. But is it cool? Will they have time for their mates, their football/soccer, rugby, hockey, basketball, netball, rock climbing and all the stuff that actually is cool?

You have convinced the school's administrators and the boss, now you have to convince the students. To be honest, it's usually a much easier job, but if you are finding it difficult to work up interest, try following some of these approaches to build anticipation, curiosity and excitement.

- Highlight both the enjoyable and enriching aspects of participating in a school play, appealing to a wide range of student interests and goals.
- Advertise the upcoming production and auditions with great pomp and ceremony.
- Have a meeting for everyone interested.
- Run a teaser campaign using posters and social media notices in newsletters/apps and the school web page etc.
- Give examples of school shows, either previous or well-known examples from movies, TV series etc.

Let's consider some recruitment techniques.

The fun reasons to get involved in your school play

- Making new friends: bond with students you may not normally meet and create lasting friendships through shared experiences.
- Being creative: express your creativity through acting, designing sets or creating costumes.
- Enjoying the spotlight: experience the thrill of performing in front of an audience and being in the spotlight.
- Dressing up: have fun wearing unique costumes and experimenting with different styles.
- Improvising: enjoy spontaneous and humorous moments during rehearsals and performances.
- Being someone else: explore diverse roles and step into the shoes of various characters.
- Learning new skills: try out different aspects of theatre production, from acting to tech work.
- Being part of a team: experience the camaraderie and teamwork involved in putting on a show.
- Getting involved in the school spirit: contribute to the school community and show your school spirit through the arts.
- Having fun during rehearsals: enjoy the process of rehearsing; it is hard work, yes, but sprinkled with plenty of laughter and memorable moments.

The more serious reasons to get involved

The ones the parents want to hear about!

- Building confidence: develop self-confidence by performing in front of an audience and receiving feedback.
- Enhancing communication skills: improve public speaking and communication skills; essential for future endeavours.
- Developing teamwork: learn to work collaboratively with others; an important skill in any career.
- Improving time management: balance rehearsals, schoolwork and other commitments, enhancing time management abilities.
- Strengthening emotional intelligence: understand and express a range of emotions, building emotional intelligence.
- Gaining leadership experience: take on leadership roles, such as directing scenes or stage managing, developing leadership skills.
- Learning responsibility: take responsibility for your role in the production, whether on stage or behind the scenes.

- Exploring cultural and historical contexts: gain insights into different cultures and historical periods through the plays' settings and themes.
- Preparing for future careers: gain experience and skills relevant to careers in the arts, entertainment and beyond.
- Academic benefits: enhance your academic profile with a well-rounded involvement in the arts, which is rightly valued in college/university applications and CVs.
- Developing critical thinking: analyse scripts, characters and performances, strengthening critical thinking skills.
- Creating lasting memories: be part of a memorable experience that will stay with you for years to come.
- Contributing to the school community: play an active role in your school's cultural life and contribute to a vibrant school community.
- Experiencing the joy of achievement: feel a sense of accomplishment from contributing to a successful production.

So you've got a *small* cast for your first production. No problem! In fact, it's probably a good thing. Starting small allows you to build a solid foundation for future shows. A small, dedicated cast is preferable to a larger, less focused one.

Being on stage isn't for everyone, but remember there's a lot more going on behind the scenes.

One more thing . . .

Remember the students have lessons, exams and other commitments. There is a whole world outside the play. What we have to strive for is a balance.

7
Performing rights and permissions

Once upon a time in a little town, near a big city, there was a young English teacher who, because they were studying the very same play in class, took his/her students to the big city to see its well-known musical version. Set in Liverpool, about twins separated at birth, it explored all the great themes like; social class, education, nature vs. nurture, growing up, fate, destiny and superstition. It blew their minds! They loved it and they wanted to do it! They knew it well for he/she was a good teacher. They also had copies of the script; they just needed to add some of those great songs! There were some decent singers in the class, so the English teacher (who was really great) asked the drama department for help and, as he/she (like many English teachers) had some lower-school drama on their timetable, the head of drama said yes! The students were over the moon. They performed to a packed audience of relatives and schoolmates for three tear-jerking nights. It was in the local paper, the talk of the town. They even made some money for the English department. It was perfect; some described it as breathtaking, others mentioned the singing and called it a triumph. The letter the school received called it unlawful and mentioned copyright theft. 'Tell me it's not true. Say it's just a story . . .'

Schools are not exempt from paying a licence fee and why should they be? These fees are what authors receive as payment for their work. You WILL need a licence if your production is public and, let's face it, 'The school play' is usually the very public face of the school. 'Public' includes anyone who is not a current student or staff member at the school, regardless of whether they buy a ticket or not and any performance occurring outside of normal school hours. (More on this later.) Don't let this put you off. Getting a licence for your school play is actually quite a straightforward process. It is often the language which can be confusing and even intimidating.

So let's simplify things.

First of all, what are performing rights?

Performing rights are the legal *permission* needed to perform a play or musical in front of an audience. Plays and musicals are protected by copyright, so you will need permission from the copyright owner to perform them publicly.

So, why do I need permission?

Copyright laws give the writer control over how their work is used and performed. Getting permission ensures that you respect the writer's rights.

Right, how do I get permission?

First, you need to identify the copyright holder (the person or persons who own the rights to the play or musical). This is usually the playwright or composer, or their publishing company. Their contact details will be within the first few pages of the script/score or can be found online. You will need to contact the rights holder and request permission. This is often easily done online. You will need to have the following information ready: play title, name of your theatre or producing organization, place of performance (town/city, state/county and name of school/theatre), seating capacity, ticket prices and whether you are a nonprofit or for-profit group (your school's status), number of performances and proposed performance dates.

Be prepared to pay a licensing fee, which could be a flat fee or may vary depending on factors like the size of your audience and what you charge for admission.

How do I know I have picked the right version?

Some plays and musicals have different versions (e.g. junior versions for younger performers). Make sure you get permission for the appropriate version that matches your performers' age and skill level.

Are there any special arrangements for schools?

Schools are often given special permissions or discounts for educational purposes. Don't forget to mention that you are from a school when requesting permission, as this can affect the cost and often simplify the process.

When should I begin the process?

You should always plan ahead and begin the permission process early, as it can take time to get approval and pay any fees. **Warning**: do not wait until the last minute before your performance date. When you get permission, keep all copies. **Warning**: authors can and do decide to restrict the availability of their plays at certain times for a variety of reasons.

What if I can't get permission for the play I want?

If you can't get permission for a particular play or musical, consider alternative works, including ones that are in the public domain or have open performance rights. Ask when the particular play will become available for future consideration.

What is the public domain?

'Public domain' means that a work is no longer under copyright protection (out of copyright), which usually happens many years after the writer's death or because they have chosen to release it into the public domain. For your school, this means you do not need to get permission to use, perform, adapt or modify the work, and you will not need to pay any royalties or fees to use the work or worry about legal restrictions and additional costs.

However, please be aware that modern translations or adaptations of older works are considered new works, with the translator or adapter owning the new copyright regardless of the date of the author's original work. For example, Molière's *Tartuffe* is out of copyright; however, McGough's adaptation is not. A good rule of thumb is that any play written before the twentieth century can be performed without a licence and all plays written from the twentieth century onwards must have a licence. However, there are exceptions, and you must always check to avoid misunderstandings.

What are the legal consequences?

Performing a play or musical without permission can lead to fines and legal action by the rights holder. These can be expensive and hugely embarrassing for you and your school.

By following these steps and being aware of your responsibilities, you can ensure a smooth and legally compliant process for putting on school plays and musicals.

Warning: for musicals, the fees to produce a work are often higher and include a rental fee (for scripts and scores). A refundable security deposit is often required. Never photocopy scripts/scores without express permission.

The name of the person who holds the rights to the play (or their representative) is usually printed on the copyright page of the book under the ominous heading, 'Caution'. Applications should be made in writing to the person/s at the address shown, or via email. Most publishers now have a website where an online application can be made. Websites also carry vital and useful information which could assist in your decision-making process.

Once you've completed and paid for your application, you'll be issued with a certificate to prove you have a licence to perform the show.

The costs of a licence varies depending on the show. It is always wise to check the play's fee on the representative's website or in writing. Exact fees depend on various factors including venue size and the price of your tickets, but an exact fee should be calculated during the application process.

If you are unable to find details of the performing rights in the text itself or you have not yet selected a script, below is a list of ten reputable performing rights search engines along with their corresponding websites.

Dramatists Play Service	https://www.dramatists.com
TRW	https://www.theatricalrights.com
Samuel French (Concord Theatricals)	https://www.concordtheatricals.com
MTI	https://www.mtishows.com
Theatrical Rights Licensing (TRL)	https://www.theatricalrights.com
Playscripts	https://www.playscripts.com
Eldridge Publishing Company	https://www.histage.com
Tams-Witmark Music Library	https://www.tamswitmark.com
Pioneer Drama Service	https://www.pioneerdrama.com
Dramatic Publishing	https://www.dramaticpublishing.com
Nick Hern Books	https://www.nickhernbooks.co.uk
Broadway Licensing	https://www.broadwaylicensing.com

These websites offer comprehensive catalogues of plays and musicals, as well as information on obtaining performance rights and licensing agreements. You can search for specific titles, browse genres, and learn about the licensing process directly on their respective websites.

Once you have obtained permission, you should carefully study all restrictions and requirements. Some are straightforward, but many of the big hits come with stipulations, which can seem odd and even a little fussy at times. Do not ignore them! Some shows will stipulate the size of the lettering of the show's name, that the writer or composer's name is prominent on tickets, billboards and press releases. Yes, this applies to schools too . . .

Remember, performing only selected scenes from your favourite show does not in any way exempt you from licensing law.

It's a common misconception that we only need a licence to perform a show if we're charging for tickets. This is far from correct! It all depends on whether your performance will be private or public. All public shows, regardless of whether or not you're charging for tickets, require a licence.

If your production is going to be private, you can perform without a licence; but be warned, private doesn't mean by invitation only or not advertised. 'Private' means that you are performing the show only for the students and staff of the school, as part of your usual school day, during normal school hours and that no invited guests from outside the school will be present. This includes parents and relatives or prospective students. In other words, nothing like a school play.

In Chapter 4, 'What's Out There?' alongside each title I give licensing details as a guide but remember some titles may have more than one agent, depending on where you are based.

One more thing . . .

A brief warning about recorded music

This is often overlooked or simply not considered, but music played before or after a performance, or during an interval, usually requires a licence from the relevant music rights organizations. Schools and educational institutions may be eligible for discounted licences, depending on the performance and the venue. However, if you plan to use copyrighted music during the production – such as recorded music within scenes or during transitions – this often requires separate permission. Standard performance licences typically don't cover this use, and you should obtain approval directly from the rights holders. Securing these rights can be complex, as there's no central system for clearing them. Often, folks tend to use copyrighted music without obtaining proper permissions, but this could lead to cease-and-desist orders or even legal action. Just saying!

8

Visions and venues

'I've done it before at my previous school so my vision is simple, it's the same as last time!' Right? Wrong!

Drawing from past experiences, one might think that replicating a previous success is a straightforward path to achieving similar results. The problem is, however, that this approach fails to recognize the unique dynamics of each new production. Whether it's a different school, a new stage, or most likely an entirely different group of students, each show presents its own set of variables. Even if it's the same show at the same school, eight years later, the cast will be different and you, as a director, will have evolved. Each new production must be approached with fresh eyes. For example, while I have directed *A Midsummer Night's Dream* and *Oliver!* many times, every iteration is a unique experience. Knowing the script and anticipating potential challenges are just the starting points; the real magic lies in exploring new possibilities with each distinct cast. Instead of striving to recreate a past success, I focus on embracing the potential that each new group brings. This allows the cast to discover and develop their own interpretations, leading to a more dynamic and original production every time.

Visions

What is an artistic vision? In the theatre, it's how we bring a play to life. From that first glimmering of an idea to how everything will look and feel on opening night.

Having a vision when organizing a school play means having a vivid and imaginative concept of how you want the final production to look, feel and resonate with the audience. This involves everything from the overall theme and tone to specific details like set design, costumes, lighting and character interpretation. It's about how you will guide the creative process with a strong sense of purpose and direction. Venues are very much tied in with your vision for the piece; this is why I deal with them in the same chapter.

The vision for every show is different, obviously, but my vision for 'The school play' has always been guided by the following principles.

At the heart of any vision I have for a production lies a commitment to selecting material that entertains, challenges and inspires. I want theatre that connects with my students and their community, exploring themes that are relevant, that matter; such as resilience, empathy and the human condition. They might be timeless dramas or modern comedies or something a little offbeat, but it's your vision as director that will make them become relevant to your students and their audience. So, when bringing a play to life, it is important to encourage collaboration and experimentation. Allow your students to take risks, explore their characters, and find their own voices as performers.

Having a clear vision of how you want the production to look and sound is crucial. Record this vision in writing, along with any sketches, drawings, or models needed to keep you and the cast/team consistently aligned with the direction of the piece.

You must generously share your vision and be open to suggestions from your design team, including, lighting, sound, set/prop design and costume. If your artistic vision for the chosen play can capture these principles, I believe even your wildest ideas can be realized on stage and be safe for students!

Venues

I confess that throughout most of my teaching career I have been blessed with good and excellent spaces for drama. However, this has not always been the case, and certainly not recently. Visiting schools in the UK and internationally, I have seen every kind of space; from absolutely stunningly, fabulous drama suites with studios, green rooms and theatres with revolving stages and hidden lighting booths, to no space at all, where performances take place in classrooms and corridors. Sadly, not all schools/colleges are created equal. The good news, however, is there is always somewhere and after all, 'This is the theatre, our audiences will believe us.' We drama teachers are experts at making the very best out what we have. We have to be!

In many ways, the school play can be traditional in every respect; in terms of material, style and venue. However, it doesn't have to be and I encourage would-be directors/producers to be willing to think outside the box. I love a traditional, full-blown musical on a big stage with band, moving lights and all the razzle we can muster, but I also try to balance this with works that are demanding in other ways, including the space.

Venturing beyond the confines of the traditional school stage, if you're lucky enough to have one, can give your productions an injection of creativity and excitement. So, even though you may be blessed with that school hall space, can you get it when you want it, and is there something out there which may enhance your work or the experiences of your students? Let's consider what else might be available.

Within the school you could consider the following.

- The gymnasium: with proper lighting and seating arrangements, a gym can serve as a versatile venue for theatrical productions.
- The cafeteria/canteen: transform the school cafeteria into a makeshift theatre with temporary stage set-ups and seating arrangements. For productions like *Bugsy Malone* or *Cabaret*, this might include tables and chairs arranged cabaret-style, where the audience sits at small tables, often with a more intimate, close-up view of the action. This layout enhances the immersive experience, making the audience feel like patrons of the speakeasy or club in the world of the show.
- Multipurpose room: many schools have multipurpose rooms that can be adapted for drama performances, offering flexibility in staging and seating arrangements.
- Lecture hall: lecture halls provide ample seating and often have built-in audiovisual equipment, making them suitable for small- to medium-sized productions.
- School library: rearranging bookshelves and furniture in the library can create an intimate setting for small-scale performances.
- Dance studio: dance studios with mirrored walls and sprung floors can offer a unique setting for performances that incorporate movement and choreography.
- Classroom: for smaller productions or staged readings, classrooms can be transformed into cozy theatre spaces, with minimal set-up required.
- Hallways or foyers: utilize hallways or foyers within the school building to stage immersive or site-specific performances, creating a unique theatrical experience for the audience.
- Drama studio or rehearsal space: if available, dedicated drama studios or rehearsal spaces within the school can be ideal for small, intimate performances, as they are already equipped with basic staging facilities.
- Art room or exhibition space: collaborate with the art department to stage performances in art galleries or exhibition spaces within the school, integrating visual art into the theatrical experience.
- School courtyard or quad: transform outdoor spaces within your school – such as courtyards or quads – into makeshift stages for open-air productions, creating a unique and memorable experience.
- Each of these alternative spaces offers its own unique atmosphere and challenges, providing opportunities for creative exploration and memorable experiences in school drama performances.

In the wider community, you could consider the following.

- Community theatre: consider renting out a local community theatre for a professional setting, equipped with advanced lighting and sound facilities, and ample seating.
- Outdoor amphitheatre: use nature's backdrop and stage your play in an outdoor amphitheatre or park; weather permitting!
- Local church or community centre: utilize auditoriums or multipurpose rooms in nearby churches or community centres. They are often available at affordable rates and equipped with basic stage facilities. See Chapter 24, 'How it Played Out' (*The Mysteries*).
- Art galleries and studios: partner with art galleries or studios to integrate visual art installations into your performance, inspiring creativity and interdisciplinary collaboration.
- Using an art gallery for a drama performance is a great celebration of creativity.
- Virtual platforms: explore virtual production options through video streaming or virtual reality environments when in-person gatherings are limited, allowing for wider audience reach while ensuring safety. See the section on film and multimedia shows in Chapter 3, 'The right stuff'.
- Site specific: this kind of staging is usually a unique site specifically adapted for the performance (often far removed from a theatre space). The choice of such staging can be linked to some kind of architectural feature or simply selected because of its everyday purpose. Some locations tie in very well with the piece being performed; for example, *Titus Andronicus* being staged in an abandoned abattoir, or *As You Like It* in a woodland (weather permitting!) Or imagine an abandoned warehouse transformed into a post-apocalyptic world for *1984* or where the echoes of its industrial past strike a chord in a production of *An Inspector Calls*.
  - Ask about using historic buildings or landmarks: partner with local historic sites such as theatres, museums or cultural landmarks to stage your play in a memorable and culturally rich environment.
  - Site-specific theatre venues are unique and neatly blur the boundaries between actor and audience. These unconventional settings breathe life into stories, lending them authenticity and resonance. Every creaking floorboard or cracked window becomes part of the performance, adding layers of meaning to the storytelling. They challenge traditional notions of stagecraft, offering a juxtaposed relationship between art and environment. Be aware, however, that each alternative venue presents its own

set of advantages and challenges, offering opportunities for creative exploration and new problems to think about. Challenges such as increased health and safety issues, or insurance for off-site performances may need to be considered. More importantly, however, the advantages of such venues are that they help to create unforgettable experiences.

Warning: with many of the great ideas listed above, it is worth remembering that rehearsals may have to take place elsewhere and then relocate to the performance space in the final days before the show. Like a professional theatre 'get-in' which although not always convenient, it does add that professional and different feel to the process.

Alternative venues are exciting and bring an added dimension, but they also create complications and considerations that you might wish to avoid during your first production.

One more thing . . .

What if your school/college isn't big enough to house or cast a play? What if there is only one teacher, or very few students or no music/drama facility?

It can be a great idea for smaller schools to collaborate with each other, join forces as it were, to produce a school play. This can bring numerous advantages, enriching the experience for students, teachers and the community. Following are some of the key benefits.

- An expanded talent pool, giving access to a more diverse range of students with skills in acting, singing, stage management and technical roles. Also, a fresh perspective will enhance creativity and innovation.
- Sharing resources will mean sharing costs too! Sets, costumes, props and equipment. The combined expertise of staff should improve the production quality.
- The broader social interaction in such a venture would involve could help build bridges and extend the community. Collaboration demands strong communication and problem-solving skills.
- There would potentially be an increased audience and revenue. Students would be exposed to a wider range of teaching skills, and a broadened perspective through cultural and creative exchange. Such ventures can help break down stereotypes and foster unity between schools and communities.
- Clearly defining roles and maintaining excellent communication through regular meetings would be essential. Transparent scheduling is crucial to prevent conflicts. Shared budgets can be a sensitive

matter, so careful planning is necessary. Ensuring the chosen material is suitable for both schools would be an early consideration. While the performance could take place at either school, it's worth considering a local community space if neither venue has adequate facilities. Your local education authority/school district may be of great assistance with such ventures.

9

Putting your team together

My hand shot up at the end of morning briefing and I blurted out the words, 'I'm going to put on a school play!'. To my surprise, the staffroom met my announcement with a wall of silent muttering, with the exception of the head of PE who had the decency to openly laugh! Another hand went up and there followed a far more interesting announcement concerning year 11's trip to a careers fair. As everyone left for their tutor groups and morning registration, a few smiled at me; one even said 'good luck', but there were definitely no takers. The head told me to 'pop in' to his office at break time as I drifted off with 7H2's register under my arm and failure on my mind.

At break time, the headmaster was far more encouraging than his staff had been that morning. He was genuinely delighted, but offered some advice on recruiting staff. His guidance came from a common sense I clearly lacked at the time. Much of what he shared, along with insights I've gathered over the years, is included in this chapter.

I think he also had a word with a of few of them; after all, a school production was why I was there. There should never be an impulsive, 'I am going to put on a school play'; it should be a well-considered '**We** are going to put on a school play.' Without a considerable team around you, you will, at the very least, wear yourself into the ground.

When you have all that energy and excitement welling up inside, it comes as a shock when you realize that not everyone in the staff room shares your enthusiasm. Some would rather boil their heads in oil and will tell you as much, whilst others may be more subtle and just look very busy or vanish into thin air when you ask for volunteers. English teachers are often willing to lend a hand, but don't assume! The highly talented music teacher may be too tied up with the choir, but they may not be the only musician in the school. Then there's the dance teacher who dislikes musicals; the part-time drama teacher who simply won't get involved in anything extracurricular; the maths teacher who is a trained choreographer, but you never asked! Staffrooms are full of surprises. The larger your school/college, the greater the scope. I've been lucky to have worked in two very large schools with many willing adults. I've also worked in very small schools, where I have been director, producer, front of house and stage manager. There are pros and cons with both; yet, however large or small your team, these are the skills you will need to possess as a group: directing, producing, designing, wood and/or metal worker, artist, lighting engineer, sound engineer, wardrobe/costumer maker/mender adaptor and facilitator, make-up artist, financial whiz kid, stage manager; and a cast to boot! If it's a musical, you will also need a musical director, rehearsal pianist, musicians, singers, dancers and a choreographer!

The advice my colleague of many years gives later in Chapter 10 seems very apt here: 'Surround yourself with people who can do the things you can't.' (M. Lovejoy, 2024.)

Luckily, the chances are that the staff room may well contain many, if not all, of these skills. Sometimes, it may not be so much a skill as a passion or interest, or even a desire to find out. All you have to do now is convince them to give up their valuable spare time and share their expertise for the next two to three months. You don't need to limit your search to the staffroom, you will be able to find a great wealth of willing talent among the parents. I always try to keep parents on side by keeping them informed. The school newsletter, or parent portals and apps will keep everyone informed of where we are at with the production, it is also a great channel for recruiting help with any number of tasks, advice, props or costume. I have recruited some wonderful, talented and willing parents over the years, even some whose children are not themselves involved like to lend a hand, a paintbrush, a saw or laptop.

Over the next six chapters, along with my advice, I am going to introduce you to sixteen exceptional people who have been involved with me in school productions in one role or another. These highly experienced and generous folk will share their accumulated wisdom and reflect upon their experiences, sharing their top tips and favourite shows. We shall look at each role in detail later, but here's a brief line-up.

With many of the roles outlined below, I refer to teams, but I am fully aware that in many cases 'team' may be one person. In which case, you must ensure that their workload is not too great.

Director	To have a vision and to run everything below. Probably going to be you.
Producer	To help facilitate the above. Probably going to be you too!
Designer	Initially you, but you must share your artistic vision for the piece with someone who can help you realize it.
Set and props	A team of skilled and willing carpenters and builders.
Artists	Talented artists to interpret your visions and a team of helpers to realize them. Probably your designer too.
Lighting	Rigging, focusing and operating a lighting desk.

Sound	Recording, mikes, sound systems and operating a sound desk.
Costume	Designer, maker, assembler, sewing and constant repairs.
Make-up	Usually there is no shortage of student volunteers, but they will need the supervision of an able and willing adult.
Front of house	An adult with a head for figures for front of house, tickets, advertising, programmes etc.
Front of house crew	Willing students/staff to see audience to seats and check tickets etc.
Advertising	To work with front of house and within the school and local community
Media people	To manage the school website and social media advertising/publicity.
A stage manager	An adult or highly disciplined older student.
Stage crew	A group of dedicated students to make the magic happen.
Admin	Applying for and adhering to performing arts rights and obligations. To manage bookings and general organization.
A cast!	Those students.
Parents	You are going to need them on board!

If it's a musical, in addition to all of the above you will also need the following: a musical director, musicians, singers, a rehearsal pianist, a choreographer and dancers.

If we consider the demands upon the first two on this list (director and producer), you will understand why you absolutely need a 'team' to assist you. Each role should be managed by a suitably qualified adult; but I always give as much of the responsibility as possible to motivated students.

So, how do you gather such a team together?

Many of these people will be on the school staff, others can be found within the parent body; you simply need to find, recruit and retain them! Governors/academy trustees are a very useful point of contact. They know people and they know the school! Word of mouth and staff meetings are a start but you can't beat social media for getting the word out there!

Gathering your team together for a school play is a crucial step in the production process. I have found the following to be very effective.

Share a post through the school's communication platforms – such as email newsletters, parent–teacher apps or social media channels – inviting staff, parents and other adults to assist with the school production. Be sure to include a list of roles and skills needed.

If you really want to go for the professional touch, put together a brief job description for each position. This is mainly aimed at the adult team, but it works well with recruiting older students. I have compiled some ideas for each skill set in Appendix D.

Host an initial meeting or information session for adults only, to introduce the play, discuss the vision and goals for the production, and outline the non-performing roles and responsibilities available for staff/parents/other adults. From this, you will be able to gauge interest and recruit participants.

Set up communication channels such as email groups/WhatsApp or other social media groups to keep everyone informed and connected throughout the production process. Regularly share updates, rehearsal schedules, deadlines and important announcements to ensure everyone is on the same page.

You will need to ensure that your team has access to the resources and support they need to succeed. This may include rehearsal spaces, technical equipment, materials for set design and costumes, funding for such expenses; and mentorship from teachers, alumni or industry professionals.

Get your site manager/caretaker/janitor onside. Involve them, make them feel needed, not simply taken for granted. You need them on your team; remember you will represent extra headaches, extra problems and yes, extra work for the site team. You need to make them feel important to the process. Because they will be.

If you are new to a school or to teaching, the following could be a useful guide as to where to begin your search for your team from the school staff.

When considering a school play and seeking assistance from colleagues, various faculties or departments can offer valuable skills. Here's a breakdown of how each might contribute.

Drama/performing arts

Skills: directing, acting, stage management, lighting, sound.
Contributions: core involvement in the production, from coaching actors to managing rehearsals and organizing the technical aspects of the performance.

English

Skills: quite often where the other drama teacher hides. After all, drama is part of English literature. Understanding and script analysis, storytelling, language.
Contributions: help with interpreting the script, understanding themes, character development, and improving dialogue or narrative structure. The best stage manager I ever worked with was an English teacher. They have that affinity with the theatre.

Music
Skills: musical direction, sound design, composition.
Contributions: composing original scores or helping students perform songs; assisting with soundtracks and effects, especially for musicals.

Art and design/visual arts
Skills: set design, props, costumes, make-up, visual aesthetics.
Contributions: designing and constructing sets, creating props, costume design and make-up application for characters.

Technology (design and technology)
Skills: woodworking, construction, electronics, lighting and mechanics.
Contributions: building sets, creating props, engineering special effects or lighting rigs and technical problem-solving for staging.

ICT/computer science
Skills: video editing, sound editing, projection, digital media.
Contributions: managing audiovisual aspects such as multimedia backdrops, video projections and sound effects; recording or live streaming performances.

Physical education (PE)
Skills: movement, choreography, coordination, physical fitness.
Contributions: assisting with choreography, fight scenes, physical movement on stage or any action sequences; training students in stage combat or dance.

Business studies
Skills: budgeting, marketing, project management.
Contributions: helping with fundraising, managing ticket sales, budgeting for the production, and marketing the play to the school and local community.

Media studies
Skills: filming, editing, media promotion, advertising.
Contributions: documenting the rehearsal process or performance, creating promotional materials such as trailers, posters or programmes. Front of house.

Maths

Skills: budgeting, logistics, scheduling.
Contributions: assisting with logistical planning, such as managing finances or devising rehearsal schedules. Front of house.

History

Skills: research, historical context, accuracy.
Contributions: offering insights into the historical period of the play, ensuring accuracy with settings, costumes and themes related to the time.

Modern foreign languages

Skills: translation, language coaching, accents.
Contributions: coaching students on accents, pronunciations, or language usage in plays set in foreign contexts; assisting with translation of scripts if needed.

Religious studies (RE)

Skills: understanding of diverse cultural/religious contexts and themes.
Contributions: providing context for plays dealing with moral, ethical or religious themes; helping students engage with sensitive material respectfully.

Psychology/sociology

Skills: understanding of human behaviour, social dynamics and character motivation.
Contributions: advising on character motivations, group dynamics, and understanding how to portray psychological or societal issues on stage.

Learning support/learning support assistant (LSA)/teaching assistant (TA)/special education (or special education department) (SPED)

Skills: staff work closely with individuals and know students very well, including what they can and cannot do.
Contributions: as you will see throughout this book, student support staff have been very much a part of every production I have ever mounted. Quite apart from their ability to get the very best from the students in their care, they often possess other skills; you just have to ask.

The rest of the school

Collaborating across these departments can greatly enhance the quality and smooth running of the production, ensuring it's a well-rounded learning experience for the students involved; and remember, there's a lot of talent in your school that may not be standing in front of a classroom; for example:

- **Caretaker/facilities manager:** they can assist with setting up the stage, moving props, and ensuring the space is safe for rehearsals and performances.
- **Administrative staff:** they can help with communications, scheduling, ticket sales, programme printing, QR codes and other logistical tasks.
- **IT staff:** they might be useful for managing sound, lighting and multimedia elements of the production.
- **School nurse/trained medic:** can assist with any first-aid needs during rehearsals or performances, and may help with medical aspects of costume and make-up (e.g. allergies).
- **Librarian:** they can assist with research related to the play, historical context, or finding scripts and reference materials.
- **Catering/kitchen staff:** they might be able to provide snacks or meals for the cast and crew during long rehearsals or performance days.
- **Marketing/PR staff:** if your school has someone responsible for communication, they can help promote the show through newsletters, social media and posters. See Chapter 13, 'Money stuff and front of house'.
- Finally, don't assume; remember that maths teacher who dances, or the history professor who fences!

One more thing . . .

I do not wish to pigeonhole any staff at your school, of course they will have many varied skills and interests outside of their subject, but appealing to their 'expertise' is both sensitive and flattering.

'Ask, and it shall be given you; seek, and ye shall find; knock, and it shall be opened unto you.' Viola, *Twelfth Night*.

10

Directors and directing

You've just survived teaching three year nine classes and one year seven, navigated a lunchtime monologue with Elowen, and taught two A-level groups back-to-back Brecht. Now, as the final bell rings, you could go home. Oh, right, 'I'm' directing the school production. Take a seat. A director's seat!

'First off, no smoke machine. Seriously, who needs a foggy stage anyway? And more green paint – yes, we're transforming the set into a jungle. The drummers under the seats? That's a lawsuit waiting to happen. And where do we put the costume rail? No, it's blocking the wings stage left; oh, and we need to rehearse that dance again, like yesterday; and Danny is in detention again, can you have a word with his teacher? Angel's mum wants a chat; apparently, she has strong feelings about next Sunday's weekend rehearsal. And where on earth are we hanging that spot? My script is still missing and now there seem to be 140 exam desks stacked on the stage, the fire brigade is here to check the exits and the lighting desk has decided to play up again! I need to leave early, start late, and possibly get a new hat because mine is too big, too small, too green and too avant-garde. Oh, and someone stole my liquorice so I'm going home.' Fantastic. So shall we start rehearsing the scene then?

It's true that directing a school play is more demanding than being a professional director on Broadway or The West End! Sounds a bit far-fetched? Consider this; it is highly likely that you will be the director and the producer! Which means you will need many, if not all of the following strengths: a theatrical knowledge, an understanding of theatrical techniques, styles and genres including stagecraft, blocking, lighting, sound and costume design. You will need to have innovative ideas for staging, blocking and interpreting the script to bring it to life on stage. It is you who will lead and inspire your cast and crew throughout the production process.

As director, you'll need to be a clear and effective communicator, able to share your vision with actors, crew members and production staff. You'll have the final say on key production elements, including props, costumes and staging details. Working with students, parents and colleagues will require strong collaboration skills, as well as the ability to coordinate schedules for rehearsals, performances and other logistical aspects of the production.

Unexpected challenges will arise during rehearsals and performances, requiring quick thinking and practical solutions. In essence, you will need the wisdom of Job and the patience of a saint. Directing a play is demanding, and not every rehearsal will run smoothly. The patience you demonstrate in the classroom will be essential after hours, as you guide students of varying abilities and experience in new contexts. Beyond patience, you must cultivate understanding and manage the emotions of cast and crew to foster a supportive and inclusive atmosphere at every rehearsal. It will be your meticulous attention to detail which will significantly enhance the overall quality of the production.

Then there's health and safety! Ensuring that rehearsals and performances are conducted in a safe manner, with proper supervision and adherence to all of those guidelines.

You are going to need to become familiar with the basic technical aspects of theatre production, such as lighting, sound, and stagecraft; even if you're not directly responsible for these areas.

Managing the finances for the production was never my strong point and with the pressure of all the other responsibilities of a director, I heartily recommend you pass the finances on to another adult. See Chapter 13, 'Money stuff and front of house'. But yes, you guessed it, ultimately you will be responsible for this too. Not to mention your own mental health! However, unlike the Broadway director, this is on top of your day job. So why would any sane person want to do it?

Mark Lovejoy

'If I left teaching tomorrow, it would be the school productions I would miss the most. It's what I'm best at.'

Mark is a lead practitioner for drama and performing arts, with whom I worked for eleven wonderful years. He has been directing school productions for twenty-one years.

'I believe school productions are important because they nurture a culture of aspiration and achievement. A nurturing community outside of the classroom, the most important things being the sense of pride and the artistry. My first childhood experience of the school production was as a drummer, I touched the drums and the audience looked around, it was the first time I realized I had an impact.'

My top tips:

'To the aspiring director, I would offer this advice: "Surround yourself with people who can do the things you can't."'

'For auditions, set the professional values high, students will come up to them. When casting, as much as possible, try to keep characters age appropriate. Rehearsals should be a purposeful working environment, in which students feel a sense of ownership and with a shared vision, work on their strengths to explore scenes. I really enjoy being creative with imagery, using projections/music to paint pictures and supplement the action of the stage.'

Favourite production I directed

'My favourite show to date has been *We Will Rock You*, just because of the quality of the principal cast and band. It was just that magic time when we had some really amazing people all in the right place at the right time which enabled us to take risks and really explore the material.'

Favourite show I've seen

'The best show I've been to the theatre to see would be *Love Song* by Abi Morgan and Frantic Assembly. The powerful use of flashbacks to convey the inescapability of time hit the audience like a sledgehammer. It left us speechless. That inevitability!'

Debbie Coad

'It is so important to give young people a platform.'

Debbie and I began our teaching careers in the same school and worked on a number of shows together. She came to my rescue on many an occasion with fresh ideas and a boundless energy. Debbie is now a subject leader for English in a multi-academy trust.

'As a child, I loved performing impromptu in front of friends and family and on stage. At primary school, drama was positively encouraged, whether through role play (the dressing-up rail was the stuff of legend) or – every Wednesday afternoon in year five – our teacher inviting us to perform for our peers; predominantly made-up plays and musicals based on the hits of Abba.'

My top tips for a new teacher facing a school show for the first time

'Get involved with whatever your school already has planned. Nothing planned? Go for it and set yourself a target of producing a play, festival or musical by the end of your second year. Don't go it alone. There will always be staff and parents who can help, and you could even have student co-director etc., to really empower them as leaders.'

'Get your performance and all the rehearsals needed onto the school calendar so there are no excuses from anyone. (a weekend rehearsal works wonders and really bonds the cast and crew, and I am certain your school would permit a dress rehearsal during the school day).'

Favourite production I directed

'*Lord of the Flies,* with amazing actors and an audience transfixed in terror and awe, with a highly visceral performance in the round.'

Favourite show I've seen

'The Propeller Company all-male cast *Twelfth Night* at the Old Vic is one students remind me about when I bump into them. Seeing sixteen-year-olds roll around laughing at Shakespeare was a real highlight. Build a culture of going to see live performance at whatever level.'

One more thing . . .

I always choose an assistant director or producer – typically a senior drama student – who can run small scene rehearsals under my supervision. Try not to let them become a glorified gofer/secretary. The role must be relevant, valued and fit the job description (see Appendix D).

11

Musical directors and choreographers

Musical director

I managed my first musical without a musical director or choreographer, surviving instead on the pity of parents, the head teacher and a governor who could play the piano. It was an experience I made sure I never repeated. Working with a good MD is vital and the more experience they have, the better. I learned a lot about directing and, yes, even about teaching, by working with some great MDs over the years.

The musical director ensures an accurate and cohesive musical performance, while the choreographer integrates movement to enhance storytelling; together, they create the artistic and technical foundation that is essential for a successful musical.

As with any role on your team, always try to engage as many students as possible; however, due to the amount of time and commitment needed during school hours, not to mention extracurricular, the musical director should be recruited from within the staff. They will be used to managing groups of students, have a knowledge of their abilities and have access to instruments.

The role of a musical director, like that of the director, is multifaceted. They too will be required to oversee the musical elements of the production and work closely with the cast, orchestra and other production staff.

Let's take a look at the responsibilities of the MD. Before rehearsals begin, the MD will need to thoroughly understand the score. This involves studying the music, understanding the vocal and instrumental parts and planning how to convey their musical vision to the performers.

The MD will need to work with the cast to teach them the songs; including working on pitch, rhythm, dynamics and articulation. They should also be involved in helping students understand the emotional context of the songs to enhance their performances. If the production includes a live orchestra or band, the MD will be responsible for rehearsing and directing them. They will need to ensure the instrumentalists understand their parts and are synchronized with the vocal performances.

The MD must work closely with the stage director and choreographer to ensure the music is allied with the staging and choreography. This will include adjusting tempo and timing, and ensuring that musical cues match the action on stage.

The MD will be in charge of running music rehearsals. This will involve teaching the music, rehearsing with the full cast, and eventually coordinating with the orchestra/band; and ensuring that everyone is comfortable and confident with their parts.

As the performance date approaches, the MD will participate in technical rehearsals, working with the sound crew to balance the levels between the orchestra and the singers, and ensuring that all musical elements are well integrated into the overall production.

In conjunction with the director and choreographer, the MD will create a comprehensive schedule that outlines all rehearsals including vocal rehearsals, orchestra/band practices and full run-throughs. An MD should consider the availability of students, especially for acting/dancing rehearsals. Stagger rehearsals to avoid burnout and ensure that students are not overwhelmed. Start with sections where small groups or individual parts are rehearsed separately, allowing focused attention on challenging sections. Gradually move to full-cast rehearsals where everyone comes together and, at this point, incorporate the orchestra or band.

An MD should outline what they want to achieve in each session – whether it's mastering a particular song, perfecting harmonies or working on a specific transition – and then communicate these goals to the cast and musicians so everyone is on the same page. While it's important to stick to a schedule, the MD must be prepared to adapt if certain areas need more attention. However, maintain firm control of deadlines and expectations, especially as the performance date approaches.

It's a great idea to provide students with rehearsal tracks so they can practice on their own. This is especially helpful for students who may need extra practice outside of scheduled rehearsals.

Warning: the MD must ensure that they schedule breaks during long rehearsals, to keep energy levels up and avoid fatigue. Regularly assess progress and address any issues immediately. This could involve extra rehearsals for specific sections or individuals who need more help.

Encourage and support students. Praise their progress and provide constructive feedback. A positive atmosphere will motivate students to give their best performance. An MD will always keep in close contact with the stage director, choreographer and technical crew to ensure that all aspects of the production are aligned. Regular production meetings are vital to keep everyone informed and on track. If you think your MD will need one, encourage them to enlist the help of an assistant MD; perhaps a senior music student with a passion for musicals (see Appendix D).

The MD (and their assistant) should always have backup plans in place for potential issues, such as key cast members being absent or technical difficulties. Flexibility and quick thinking will be essential as the production progresses.

Let's put all of that into a list!

- Musical preparation:
    - Thoroughly study and understand the score before rehearsals begin.
    - Familiarize yourself with vocal and instrumental parts.
    - Plan how to convey your vision for the music to the performers.
- Rehearsal planning:
    - Create a comprehensive schedule with all rehearsals, including vocal, orchestra practices, and full run-throughs.
    - Consider student availability and balance acting/dancing rehearsals to avoid burnout.
    - Begin with small group or individual rehearsals for challenging sections.
    - Gradually move to full-cast rehearsals and then incorporate the orchestra.
    - Outline session goals (e.g. mastering songs, perfecting harmonies) and communicate them clearly.
    - Be prepared to adapt the schedule as needed, while maintaining deadlines and expectations.
- Teaching and coaching:
    - Work with the cast to teach songs; focusing on pitch, rhythm, dynamics and articulation.
    - Help students understand the emotional context of their songs to enhance performances.
    - Provide rehearsal tracks for students to practice independently.
- Orchestra direction:
    - If applicable, rehearse and direct the live orchestra.
    - Ensure that instrumentalists understand their parts and are synchronized with the vocal performances.
- Collaboration:
    - Work closely with the stage director and choreographer to align music with staging and choreography.
    - Adjust tempos, timing and ensure musical cues match the action on stage.
    - Keep in close contact with the technical crew to ensure all aspects of the production are integrated.
- Music rehearsals:
    - Run music rehearsals, including teaching, rehearsing with the full cast and coordinating with the orchestra.

- Ensure that everyone is comfortable with and confident about their parts.
  - Schedule breaks during long rehearsals to maintain energy levels and avoid fatigue.
- Technical rehearsals:
  - Participate in technical rehearsals to work with the sound crew.
  - Balance sound levels between the orchestra and singers.
  - Ensure that all musical elements are well integrated into the overall production.
- Assessment and adaptation:
  - Regularly assess progress and address issues immediately.
  - Hold extra rehearsals if needed for specific sections or individuals.
  - Encourage and support students, providing constructive feedback and praise.
- Backup plans and flexibility:
  - Develop backup plans for potential issues such as cast absences or technical difficulties.
  - Be flexible and ready to adapt as the production progresses.
- Administrative tasks:
  - Maintain records of rehearsals, attendance, and progress.
  - Communicate effectively with students, parents and other stakeholders.

Jennie Pitman

'Kids love a whole-school musical. It quite literally is the time of their lives, where they discover themselves in a different light.'

Jennie leads a large performing arts department and has been a musical director for school productions for more than twenty-four years. We have worked together on six musicals.

'I remember being in year seven and signing up for *Joseph*, but lost my nerve and literally ran out of the audition. Later when I watched the show I was filled with remorse. For the following six years, I involved myself in the band as a pianist. It wasn't until year thirteen, when I realized it was my last chance to perform onstage, that I auditioned for *My Fair Lady*. I got the part of Mrs Pearce, I had a solo song and I loved it.'

My top tips

'Ensure you communicate a shared vision with the director. Allow plenty of rehearsal time and learn the songs first and keep revisiting them! They will forget them. For first auditions pick a well-known song (an original from the show if possible); put it on Google classroom for everyone who wants to audition. In groups of five they sing – together at first – and you listen with your yes/no/maybe head on. Then they sing individually and you prepare your callbacks list. Produce a large spreadsheet listing the character, song and scene run order! Rehearse the singers and band together as soon as possible. In those rehearsals, if at all possible, do NOT be the pianist; you conduct! If you are going to use a student band, enlist the help of peripatetic staff, get the instrument teachers involved in teaching students their parts.'

Favourite show I directed

'It has to be *Oliver!* It's challenging without being too difficult, it has great songs, loads of parts both main and ensemble, so lots of students can get involved. The band parts are well written, everyone knows the story, lots of opportunities for dance numbers and the students really love it.'

Favourite show I've seen

'My favourite show to watch has always been *We Will Rock you.*'

Gwawr Mills

'The opportunity to be in the limelight. For their parents they are the star.'

Gwawr was head teacher of a Welsh primary school for twenty years. Her specialism is music.

'My first experience of school productions was watching my mother's school rehearsals. I was in concerts and performing from an early age, mainly church stuff. In my own school (primary) our shows tended to be based around the nativity, Noah's ark etc.'

My top tips

'Make sure they know the words to the songs first; the minute they start acting and dancing, they tend to forget. Don't sweat the small stuff, at primary school, they will wave to mum and dad! Keep scenery safe and simple with plenty of adults backstage. Use repetitive words/songs for the little ones who can't yet read.'

Favourite show I directed

'As music director, it would have to be a variety of pantomimes (*Humpty Dumpty* and *Dick Whittington*) due to the interaction with the audience, and how this keeps this tradition alive. Many children these days don't know traditional songs and nursery rhymes. Great for pupils to be a part of the cast singing/dance and acting; a great grounding for any child with dreams of stardom.'

Favourite show I've seen

'*Joseph* by Andrew Lloyd Webber. The songs are amazing and Tim Rice's words are so clever. It's worth mentioning that *Joseph* was also written for school children, so is very accessible. I've used it in RE/music/drama/dance cross-curricular. Children understand it, and it is a vehicle to many genres of music.'

The choreographer

I was lucky in that my first musical wasn't full of big dance numbers. *Sweeney Todd* is really much more focused on the dramatic narrative and musical score than any complicated dance routines. The few choreographed segments in the school edition were simple and about enhancing the dramatic tension rather than showcasing dance; supporting the storyline and character interactions, rather than being stand-alone dance numbers. Fortunately, as I'm no dancer! My second musical, however, was *Oliver!*

I have used older students who are proficient dancers, to great effect, but it is good to have an adult in overall charge. The choreographer will be responsible for creating and teaching the choreography for all dance sequences in the show. They will need to understand the style of the music, the abilities of the students and the overall vision of the show.

Beyond dance, a choreographer can also help with staging certain scenes, ensuring that actors move fluidly across the stage, and transitions are smooth. They will work closely with the director to ensure that the choreography aligns with the shared vision; this will involve discussions about the tone, pacing and style of the different scenes.

They will need to coordinate with the musical director to ensure that the choreography matches the musical timing, and with the director to integrate dance with the acting performances. The role involves teaching the dance routines to the students, breaking down movements step by step, and ensuring that all students, regardless of skill level, feel confident in their performance. It also requires giving constructive feedback, helping students refine their movements, improve their technique and build confidence on stage.

The choreographer will run rehearsals dedicated to dance, working with the students to perfect each routine and ensure that it fits seamlessly into the show. Then, as the production progresses, they will integrate the dance rehearsals into full-cast rehearsals; helping to ensure that the dancing, acting and singing come together cohesively.

Part of the role will be to encourage and motivate students, especially those who might be less confident in their dancing abilities. There will be challenges such as varying skill levels, time constraints or unexpected changes, and your ability to adapt and keep the students engaged will be key.

As the production date nears, the choreographer will need to be present at dress rehearsals, to ensure that costumes and props don't interfere with their choreography, and make any final adjustments. During the actual performances, the best place for the choreographer is backstage, assisting students with quick changes, calming nerves and making sure the dance routines go off without a hitch.

That handy list:

- Choreography creation and teaching:
    - Create and teach the choreography for all dance sequences in the show.
    - Understand the style of the music, the abilities of the students and the overall vision of the show.
- Scene staging and transitions:
    - Help with staging certain scenes to ensure actors move fluidly across the stage.
    - Ensure transitions between scenes are smooth.
- Collaboration with director:
    - Work closely with the director to align the choreography with their vision.
    - Discuss the tone, pacing and style of different scenes with the director.
- Coordination with musical director:
    - Coordinate with the musical director to ensure choreography matches the musical timing.
    - Integrate dance with acting performances in collaboration with the director.
- Teaching and refining:
    - Teach dance routines to students, breaking down movements step by step.
    - Ensure all students, regardless of skill level, feel confident in their performance.
    - Provide constructive feedback to help students refine movements, improve their technique and build confidence.
- Dance rehearsals:
    - Run rehearsals dedicated to dance, perfecting each routine.
    - Integrate dance rehearsals into full-cast rehearsals as the production progresses.
    - Ensure that dancing, acting and singing come together cohesively.
- Student encouragement:
    - Encourage and motivate students, especially those less confident in their dancing abilities.

- Adapt to challenges such as varying skill levels, time constraints or unexpected changes. Identify talented/trained student dancers and get them involved in teaching routines to the cast.
- Dress rehearsals:
    - Be present at dress rehearsals to ensure costumes and props do not interfere with choreography.
    - Make final adjustments as needed.
- Performance assistance:
    - Assist backstage during performances, helping with quick changes and calming nerves.
    - Ensure dance routines go off without a hitch during actual performances.

Kirsty Edwards-Longhurst

'It isn't just dancing, it's acting through movement.'

I was, for a number of years, very lucky to work with a professional choreographer who would come in to school and help during the production week. Kirsty has been dancing since she was four. She was a student teacher at her dance school from the age of fourteen and was national tap dance champion in the UK. She went on to work as a professional choreographer in Bollywood and pantomime, as well as on cruise ships and at dance schools. She is now qualifying as a psychodynamic psychotherapist, aiming to help young dancers and performers cope with the pressures of competition and body image. 'The mind is part of the body.'

'My first show at school was *The Nativity*. I didn't get to speak, but I was literally the star and the cast had to follow me everywhere on stage. In my last year at secondary, I played Rizzo in *Grease*; a part dear to my heart.'

My top tips

'Get to know the director and how they work. Get to grips with all of the music. Listen to it, study it. Learn the characters. Look around; it's ok to watch film of other productions of the show. Learn the show. Get your notebook out and plan! Plan ahead. Get to know the cast, how many in each routine. Listen to the music and write your eights down. Be organized!

Never walk into a rehearsal without a step in your brain or on your notepad! Be prepared.

Really get to know the performers. Who is comfortable with what? Who are the dancers and movers? And work this into your notes. Make them feel comfortable. Be confident in rehearsals, supportive but pass on a confidence. Never be a scary choreographer, there's nothing worse.'

For auditions

'For me the best way to audition for dancers in a school (if you have time), is by year group. This way they are with their peers and less intimidated. Audition in lines but move front to the back and rotate as you teach the routines. This way, everyone gets to see you. Teach a couple of eights then move them to the back etc. Start with simple routines and build in the difficulty throughout the routine. Give time for practice for everyone to get it; in the audition, see one line at a time and let them do it twice. This way, they get a chance to improve under pressure. Keep the audition upbeat and vibrant. The energy levels must be kept high throughout. Finish on a high, all together, perhaps allow them to freestyle the number. Thank them, appreciate their effort: "You've been amazing." Dismiss them and sit down with the director!'

Favourite production I choreographed

'My favourite shows to choreograph have always been about the glitz and glam, so shows like *42nd Street*. However, my all-time favourite – and this surprised me – was *The Pirates of Penzance!* I loved the satirical humour.'

Favourite show I've seen

'The best thing I ever saw has to be *Cabaret* on Broadway with Alan Cumming as the MC. It was an unforgettable masterclass for me!'

Nikki Dobbs

'It's all about the kids. The show gives them a breathing space.'

Nikki has been dancing since she was three. She has been choreographing school shows for the last ten years. A dancer, housemistress and drama teacher, we have worked together on three shows.

My top tips

'Keep auditions simple, and unintimidating as possible. Don't overcomplicate routines, get them sharp! Like any lesson, you should differentiate your choreography. You may be professionally trained, they are usually not. Simplify it and take it from there. With younger students, don't be afraid to cut a number short. Short, sharp, fast and effective! Use improv. What does a piece mean to them? Students learn from having the space to be creative under your guidance and feedback. Always stick to schedules and NEVER overrun.'

Favourite productions I choreographed

'*Little Shop of Horrors* and *Honk* for the younger ones. But the best was Kneehigh's *Tristan and Yseult*. The story of heartbreak and passion enabled me to create some very moving, slow physical pieces. The show is so diverse, with great changes of rhythm as the story develops. Such a challenge.'

Favourite show I've seen

'That would have to be Kneehigh's *Rebecca* at the National. I loved the darkness of it, the sense of mystery and the storytelling!'

12

Designing and making your set and props

In the back of my first director's script, among the production notes, lay a diagram with instructions for constructing Sweeney Todd's chair. It included several options for the fiendish contraption, from sliding seats and pivots to simple blackouts. As we had a service area below the stage, I decided to use the trapdoor and immediately set about designing a complicated device that slid victims down at a steep angle. The technology department started building it, while I explored the area beneath the stage. The space under the stage was shocking; crammed with twenty years of school debris, including broken chairs, blackboards, tangled venetian blinds, a surprising quantity of half-eaten sandwiches and about 700 hymn books, liberally sprinkled with rat droppings. When I asked the caretaker where I should put it all, he provided some anatomically impossible suggestions and told me nothing could be thrown away. So it stayed, lunches included, and as we didn't require Sweeney's victims to die each night, we sealed the hatch and left it to the rats. Then began the search for an alternative, involving dangerous experiments with chairs that shot the occupant backwards in a neck-breaking arc, one which required the victim to crawl out of the back; and yet another which sort of collapsed flat, leaving the potentially fingerless victim to roll out under a stage block. We finally opted for a chair with wheels, a curtain and a blackout. I was disappointed, but no students or rats were harmed.

Today, you can find any number of videos on YouTube explaining precisely how to build Sweeney's chair. I strongly recommend you watch a few of them. In fact, whatever your chosen text, there are thousands of helpful tutorials with brilliant ideas on making good, solid sets, props and costumes for the stage in general.

Whatever the play, whatever your vision, experience has taught me that directors are prone to underestimating the sheer amount of 'stuff' they're going to need. Do we have a typewriter? Can we borrow a spinning wheel? Can you buy half a car? Does anyone know how to make a toy dog look real and move, but not be laughed at? How can we make a cut-throat razor safe? Does anyone have a First World War gas mask lying around that they don't need? I need ten functioning splurge guns, including one which fires backwards. Or conversations such as: 'Yes, I wonder if you can help, we need to borrow one of your coffins; no, we only need it for a three days; oh, hang on, and a weekend rehearsal.'

Sooner or later, someone will need to take on the task of acquiring or creating 'stuff'. Give them the time they need! Asking for a fully functioning, yet safe guillotine takes time, even with the internet! There are many wonderful groups on social media run by and dedicated to drama and the unending search for all things theatre; from props and sets to scores, scripts and advice. If you're needing something specific, do try these first, they can be a lifesaver. Even if they don't have what you're looking for, the collective mind will usually know where you can get that elusive prop, or how to make it. Being part of one of these groups is a mutually beneficial experience. Sharing advice, props, sets or simply offering reassurance has become an invaluable resource for everyone involved in community theatre. Also consider freecycle sites and local charity shops. For everything else, you will have to make it!

So, my advice is always to keep it to a minimum! However, with even the most minimalist of visions, you should consider the following.

Set

Much of the basic building blocks of the set may already be part of the drama department's resources. But not always.

- Backdrops: painted or printed scenery. Available to buy single/double-sided for painting or projecting upon. Versatile and reusable, a good investment for your department.
- Flats: vertical structures such as walls (built from wood or cardboard).
- Doors, entrances/exits: can be bought or constructed. (the lighter the better).
- Platforms: raised stage levels. If budget permits, consider buying, as levels are a good investment for any drama department. They can be made, but do consider durability, purpose and, of course, safety.

Props

- Handheld items: objects such as books, cups; really it's just a case of asking around or visiting charity shops.
- Furniture: tables, chairs, benches. Such larger items can still be sought locally through the school community and local charity shops, Freecycle etc. Borrow, buy or make.

- Specialty props: unique items specific to the play (make or source). If you are considering keeping them after the show, do consider space!

Set designers, artists and builders

It is only fair that any person/persons being asked to volunteer for your designer/builder team is aware that the following demands will be made of them.

They will be required to collaborate and work closely with the director (you) to ensure that you have a shared vision for the production. Depending on the setting and time period of the play, the design team may need to do some research to ensure their designs look authentic.

They will need to work to deadlines and be flexible and able to make adjustments and revisions to the design concepts as the rehearsal process progresses and new ideas emerge. They will need to collaborate effectively with other production teams, such as the stage crew and costume department, to ensure integration of all elements on stage.

If members of the design team have specialized technical skills such as set construction, allow them to utilize their expertise to enhance the production.

Probably as important as carpentry skills will be the need for artistic sensibility; that is, an understanding of aesthetics and design principles to create visually appealing sets and props that enhance the storytelling of the play.

Resourcefulness is vital, being able to work within budget constraints and make the most of available resources, whether it's repurposing materials or finding cost-effective alternatives.

When you recruit your team of set designers, you should ensure that you have at least one person who will be able to realize your vision. (In my experience, this is often the art teacher). A person who is willing to read the script and listen to and discuss your ideas on how the whole thing should look. I have always found that a shared vision with the designer is the key to a successful, believable set. Together, you should consider: the time period, location and thematic elements of the play to inform your design choices. During the rehearsal process, ideas often evolve and change. However, it's important to bear in mind that once a set is designed and built, it becomes less adaptable. Therefore, a key feature should be flexibility of interpretation. In this regard, simple sets are best. You should also be aware that continually making adjustments to the original concept/vision will increase the set designer and builders' workload and almost certainly increase their costs. Ideally, your set designer will be able to coordinate the construction of scenic elements such as platforms, walls, doors and furniture with an eye to scale, proportion, functionality and safety in order to create a visually compelling environment on stage.

In addition, your set design team will be required to select and source props and furnishings to enhance the authenticity of the set. This may entail designing custom props or modifying existing items to suit the needs of the production. Set design plays a crucial role in creating the immersive world of the play, providing a visual backdrop that enhances the storytelling. As you can see, you are going to be asking a lot of your set design team; remember they are volunteering to help you. Treat them well at all times!

The art teacher

My first port of call when sharing my vision has always been the art teacher. As a set designer, they help develop your ideas and vision for the play, they provide guidance on specifics and help keep you grounded when attempting to realize your whole vision on stage.

The art teacher's expertise in painting and creating backdrops that set the scene and establish the atmosphere is vital. Tapping into their creative expertise and artistic sensibility will enhance the visual elements of the production. Listen to them! They are also best placed to recruit student artists to help.

It can be great fun to work with the art department on the promotion of the play within the school community and further afield by creating visually engaging posters, banners, displays and digital art to generate excitement and interest in the production. The art department can run competitions to get the best ticket designs, programme cover and posters. You may, however ,have equal support from business studies and ICT faculties in the promotion of the play.

Jonathan Hamblin

'The school show is the arts faculty's sports day. This is why we teach art, dance, music and drama. The show demonstrates how the arts link together and involve many skills. A school would be a dull place without it.'

Jonathan was head of art and has worked on whole-school productions including *Rock Challenge,* and Shakespeare festivals for over thirty years.

'I went to an all-boys school, so naturally my first role in a school play was as a woman. I had one line, which was a loud scream. I didn't like being on stage, but enjoyed the inclusivity of it. I never got on stage again, but I was always there to paint it, to design and realize visions.'

My top tips

'If this is your first show, don't take on too much. You need to be given time by the school – chunks of time – not half an hour here and twenty minutes there. Time to set up, and time to clean up afterward. Involve a small group of trusted students. Be aware of department politics: are you spending too much time helping drama? You should have a shared vision with the director, not just a rushed meeting. Something on paper. The director should welcome your input; it shouldn't be simply colouring in their ideas. You should expect a budget for materials. You absolutely cannot be expected to use your department's poster colours and brushes.'

Favourite show I've been involved in

'*Oliver!* A part of something vast, yet a team within a team. My team was not on stage, but we were just as proud of our achievements.'

Favourite show I've seen

'*The Woman in Black*. A whole-theatre experience. Very scary, with such great atmospheric set design.'

One more thing . . .

Prioritize durability and simplicity in set and prop design, using lightweight, reusable materials that are easy to repair, transport and store.

13

Money stuff and front of house

I was up to my neck in double cast rehearsals, a melted lighting rig, cast members mysteriously vanishing, fire brigade checks, negotiations with my friend the surly caretaker, and redesigning the tilt mechanism for Sweeney's chair for the fourth time when someone asked if I'd given any thought to the ticket design. Then it struck me. Oh yeah, an audience! It wasn't that I was completely stupid, I was just doing too much!

But it was a point, what about an audience? My philosophy is that we should charge for tickets, but at an affordable rate; that it should balance our expenses and modestly support the arts/drama programme of the school. I further believe that not all money raised from the show needs to come from ticket sales. There is one abiding rule and that is: prior to confirming the show selection, you have to sit down and list the estimated expenses (see balance sheet section below), and then re-calculate that the actual expenses will surpass those initial estimates. You must then work out a plan that will ensure you will be capable of at least covering all of those costs. To this end, selling all of your tickets is important, but it doesn't end there.

In the beginning, I didn't have such a philosophy; in fact, I didn't have a clue! My first encounter with a 'budget' came when I ordered twenty-five copies of the script for *Sweeney Todd* and the bursar enquired from which 'budget' the money was to be taken. I was clueless and remember thinking, 'What budget? Do I have to buy them?' Then there was the rental of the score, and again the bursar quite rightly wanted to know what this was going to cost and who would be paying for it? It was all very confusing; I was a drama teacher and now the director of our school show. What I certainly was not, was a financial wizard, or a financial anybody! But I learned. I learned quickly that producing a school show, especially a musical, incurred significant expenses and it seemed everyone wanted a piece of my non-existent budget. Eventually, the money was 'found' and 'allocated', as a 'loan' for the show with the stipulation that it would need to pay for itself. Happily, there were folks in the school, including the bursar, and from the wider community who understood money and showed me how it all worked. By my third production, I had become pretty proficient at making school theatre self-funding.

So, you convinced the boss to let it happen; you fully cast the show with multitudes of willing students; you even have a crew! Now we need the show to be a sell-out, for every performance.

My tips

1. We need to go right back to the beginning of the process to ensure success. Choose the right play for your school and community (see Chapter 3).
2. Recruit a passionate and reliable team of students, teachers and volunteers for the various front of house roles.
3. Create a budget on paper.
4. Ticket prices should represent good value whilst balancing your costs.
5. Develop a comprehensive marketing strategy including timelines and responsibilities.
6. Advertising really starts around the time you begin first auditions. The students will be talking about it around the school and certainly at home, so it's not too soon to be getting the message out there, even if it's just to get the dates in the calendar.
7. Throughout the rehearsal time you should be building your advertising campaign with eye-catching posters around the school. Design visually appealing posters and flyers and digital art that showcase the play's title, date, time, venue and key details. Use vibrant colours, engaging graphics and clear typography to grab attention.
8. Use school communication platforms, such as email newsletters, parent–teacher apps or social media channels, both with parents and within the school.
9. Utilize social media platforms such as Facebook, Instagram, X (Twitter) and TikTok to promote the play. Create event pages and, as the rehearsals progress, share behind-the-scenes photos and videos, post sneak peeks, cast interviews and engage with your audience through interactive content. **Warning:** be sure to adhere to school policies when posting!
10. Engage with local media by sending a press release to local newspapers and radio stations to gain coverage.
11. Get your media department/students to create a short, engaging video trailer and share it widely. Again, be aware of school protocols on posting content containing images of students.

12. Partner with local businesses for sponsorships, discounts, and cross-promotions.
13. I always have a pre-sale for cast cast/crew family and friends.
14. Offer group discounts.
15. Encourage parents and alumni to attend and spread the word.
16. Consider using online ticketing. There are dedicated school ticketing systems available; or even tailor your own. Or you could consider using a QR code system.
17. Set up a physical 'box office' within the school to sell tickets at break and lunchtimes and other school gatherings.
18. Design a professional programme with cast bios and interesting facts about the play. Sell advertising space with local businesses. Acknowledge your sponsors in the programme.
19. Provide refreshments (however, see notes on 'the sweet wrapper rustlers' in Chapter 23).
20. Always thank your audience.
21. Review everything you did – what worked and what didn't – seek audience, colleague and student feedback. See the section on 'looking back and planning forward' in the concluding chapter.

Your essential balance sheet

Expenses	**Income**
The things that will cost you money	*The things that will earn you money*
Script purchase or rental	Ticket sales
Score purchase or rental	Programmes
Materials and set construction	Advertising within programme
Props, purchase or hire.	Sponsorship
Costume making/renting/buying	Existing budget
Marketing	Merchandise and concessions.
Possible venue rental/costs	
Sundries	
TOTAL	TOTAL

It's important to consider both the order in which the money will be spent and when it will come in.

Carefully plan and manage your expenses. Keep track of every aspect of production costs, including scripts/score, licensing fees, venue rental, costumes, props and marketing expenses. Look for cost-effective options without compromising the quality of the production. (For example, look for used copies of scripts when possible).

Warning: do not be tempted to photocopy scripts. It's illegal!

Invest time and resources into promoting your show effectively. Utilize various marketing channels such as social media, posters, flyers, email newsletters and school announcements to reach a wide audience. Partner with local businesses or organizations for cross-promotion opportunities.

Engage with the local community to generate interest and support for your show. Encourage students, teachers and parents to spread the word and attend the performance. Consider hosting special events related to the production to attract more audience members. Seek sponsorship from local businesses, corporations or individuals who are willing to support the production financially in exchange for advertising in the programme or other form of recognition. Consider partnering with community theatres, arts organizations, or educational institutions to share resources and reduce costs.

Organize post-show fundraising activities such as cast meet-and-greets, auctions or benefit concerts to continue generating revenue even after the main performance.

Look at the ticket pricing step-by-step strategy below, which describes how you can create a ticket pricing plan that supports your production costs, balancing the need to cover costs and possibly raise funds whilst ensuring accessibility for the school community.

What is it going to cost?

Calculate the total cost of producing the play, including costumes, sets, lighting, sound, marketing and any other expenses. (Leave nothing out, no matter how small.)

Decide if the primary goal is to break even, make a profit for future productions, or raise funds for the drama department.

Who is going to be paying?

Consider the economic demographics of your school community to set an affordable price point.

Estimate the potential number of attendees to ensure pricing aligns with expected turnout. How many seats can you safely fit in the space? How many seats do you physically have?

Determine pricing

General admission: set a standard ticket price for most attendees. Discounted tickets: offer discounted tickets for students, senior citizens and possibly for advance purchases.

Offer group rates and packages

Provide discounts for families purchasing multiple tickets. Offer reduced rates for groups, such as school clubs or community organizations.

Advanced sales

Encourage early purchases with a slight discount to help gauge attendance and ensure better financial planning. Cast sales.

Marketing and communication

Clearly communicate the ticket prices and any available discounts through all school and community channels. Promote the play and ticket sales through school newsletters, social media, the school website/app and local community boards. When getting your message out there through social media, involve students. They usually know at least twice as much as we do about what gets noticed and what doesn't!

Which brings us neatly to the front of house team.

Front of house manager and team

This area provides a number of great opportunities for business studies students and their teachers to become involved in a school show in a professional, hands-on fashion. The front of house manager and their team play a crucial role in ensuring the smooth operation of a school production from the perspective of the audience.

Following are the key responsibilities of the front of house manager and their team.

- Box office management: coordinating ticket sales and reservations, handling enquiries from patrons, and managing ticketing systems or box office software to ensure an organized and efficient ticketing process.

- Ushering: recruit, train and supervise ushers who assist patrons with finding their seats, distributing programmes, and providing information about the venue and the production.
- Providing a welcoming and hospitable environment for patrons, including ensuring accessibility for patrons with disabilities, assisting with seating accommodations, and addressing any special requests or concerns.
- The team will also have the very important task of maintaining a safe and secure environment for the audience by implementing crowd management procedures, monitoring entrances and exits, and responding to any emergencies or incidents that may arise during the performance.

An extra way of raising funds is to run a concessions stand during the interval of the show. The responsibility for concessions such as snacks and beverages and even merchandise such as souvenirs or cast recordings would also fall to the front of house team.

The front of house manager would be required to train their front of house team to provide good customer service, including greeting patrons with a friendly smile, addressing any concerns or complaints promptly and professionally, and ensuring that patrons have an enjoyable experience at the production. This is all great training for careers in leisure and tourism.

After the show is over, the team can assist with post-performance activities such as audience surveys or feedback collection, cleanup and resetting of front of house areas, and coordinating with the production team for any post-show events or receptions.

Many of these people will be on the school staff, others can be found within the parent body; you simply need to find, recruit and retain them! Governors/academy trustees are a very useful point of contact. They know people and they know the school! Word of mouth and staff meetings are a start, but you can't beat social media for getting the word out there!

Janette Anderson

'Being part of the front of house for a school show just brings everything together; it makes it all relevant, from the dancers, singers and actors to the lessons in my computer room.'

Janette is head of computer science and has been involved in the front of house operations of school shows for seven years. Her first experience of front of house was selling refreshments during the interval.

My top tips

'Use the more confident students for ushering, meeting and greeting. Use spreadsheets for seating plans or use some of the great software out there.

Try to get involved in the ticket designs; this is often done by the art department, along with the posters but don't be afraid to offer some designs. Students dealing with ticket sales need to be good with maths. Ticket sales must be controlled by an adult and recorded meticulously to avoid overselling and seating mix-ups.'

Favourite show I was involved in

'*Grease*, because both of my children were in it.'

Favourite show I've seen

'*Billy Elliot*, for the laughter and the tears!'

One more thing . . .

Schools and colleges operate like businesses, so to gain support, it's essential to show a willingness to manage your show's finances in a similar way.

14

Sound and light and all things technical

During four years of teacher training, I learned about the theatre and how to teach it to teenagers. At no point on my course was I ever encouraged to even look at a lighting rig or sound desk. I once entered the university's 'tech room' and though the smell of coffee and farts didn't dissuade me, the two guys in there were so very odd in that slightly unpleasant, rather rude dude way, that I decided to leave the techie stuff to the odd couple.

To be fair, everything the university produced was expertly lit and always sounded very professional; they just never shared how they did it and we just took the magic for granted. It was about five weeks before my first show, at my first school, was about to open when it occurred to me that it might be nice to light and amplify it. Why did I leave it so late? Simple answer, I was too busy and it never occurred to me to ask for help or advice. So I asked and was directed toward a pair of ancient, school-issue wooden wardrobes towering unnoticed at the other end of the hall. Since it was the caretaker doing the 'pointing', I figured he'd be just the chap to ask about keys for the large padlocks guarding the treasures within. 'Don't ask me, mate', he actually laughed; then left.

The following morning, I asked around in the staffroom but nobody knew or cared. So, with four desperate weeks left before *Sweeney Todd* opened, with the aid of a large screwdriver I broke the first lock off in a fit of wood-splintering desperation. Inside was a hinged fold-out plank of wood which nearly amputated both my arms as it crashed to the floor. I stood and looked at my handiwork. The splintered wood, still-closed padlock and the hidden booby trap now lying on the floor were a bit incriminating! The shelves were filled with what looked like the contents of the Tardis. Then I noticed a post-it note. Written on it were the magical words, 'Need help? Phone Stuart', and a number. I called it and Stuart was at my side in what seemed like minutes. An ex-student who had been the school's techie since childhood, he'd stuck the post-it there when he moved on three years ago; and I was the first to call! To me, he was nothing short of a miracle; he made every ancient appliance in the cupboard work. He even explained how the lump of wood that had almost cut off my arm, when used properly, could fold out neatly into a sound and light desk. It even had little folding legs which still worked, after he'd repaired them for me. He then solved the mystery of the blue scaffolding chained to the wall as he unlocked another padlock (he actually had the keys on his keyring) and folded out a vast, decrepit scaffold tower. He muttered something about it not being very safe and proceeded to hang every light we were going to need and even used something called safety chains! He came in on two full-weekend rehearsals and, with an arsenal of spares and gaffer tape, saw to it Sweeney was lit and miked as professionally as anything my university had ever done. Stuart was one of those souls every lonely drama teacher needs. He cherished every piece of equipment, lovingly coaxing it all to life. He even trained a group of year eight students who had shown an interest in the strange world of the techie and handed over his keys to them when the time was right.

Years later, the caretaker went on a course entitled 'Working at heights.' Armed with his new knowledge, the first thing he did was consign the old lighting tower to the scrap heap, rendering our rig unreachable for eleven long months before the school budget stretched to a new tallescope. It took about an hour to set up by the newly trained caretaker who had since become a site manager. He was also, coincidentally, the only person in the county allowed to use it. Or so he told me.

Some schools/colleges may be blessed with a theatre technician who will supervise sound and lighting for shows and public events. It would still be a wonderful opportunity for many students to become involved.

Lighting and sound techies

Although these roles are often combined, it is great to involve two students and share the creative experience, perhaps under the care of a member of staff or experienced older student.

The lighting technician plays a crucial role in enhancing the visual impact and atmosphere of a play. Techies are often found within the student body, but it is still a wise idea to have a technology expert (or similarly skilled adult) to oversee this post. Their key roles and responsibilities would be as follows.

Lighting design: collaborate with the director and other members of the production team to create a lighting design that complements the overall vision of the play. This involves determining the placement, colour, intensity and timing of lights to enhance mood, highlight key moments, and create visual interest on stage. Once the design is in place, the next task is to plot the lighting; this outlines the placement of each lighting fixture and the cues for when they should be activated throughout the performance. This serves as a blueprint for programming the lighting console and executing the cues during rehearsals and performances. This then needs to be programmed, usually through a lighting console to control the lights according to the lighting plot. A part of this is creating cues for different scenes, transitions and special effects; as well as adjusting the parameters of individual lights (e.g. intensity, colour, focus) as needed.

Warning: it is imperative that all lighting equipment is installed, operated, and maintained in accordance with safety regulations and best practices to minimize the risk of accidents or injuries. Students should not be used to hang lights from heights (see 'Job descriptions for your production team', (Appendix D). But staff should consult the school's Health and Safety policy.) and anyone who is engaged in this should be trained in working at heights. Adults so trained can then assist with the set-up and installation of lighting equipment; including hanging and focusing lights, running cables, and ensuring that all fixtures are properly connected and functioning.

Warning: it's also worth mentioning to your eager young assistants sat at the lighting desk, that absolutely no drinks are ever allowed anywhere near this vital equipment!

As the rehearsals enter the later stages, your techies should join the process to fine-tune the lighting cues and make adjustments based on feedback from the director, performers and other members of the production team. This may involve experimenting with different lighting effects, angles and colours to achieve the desired look and feel for each scene.

Your student techie can then operate the lighting console during performances to execute the lighting cues according to the timing and sequence established in the lighting plot. This requires attentiveness, precision and the ability to react quickly to changes in the action on stage. All of the team should be prepared to troubleshoot any technical issues or malfunctions that arise with the lighting equipment during rehearsals or performances. This may involve troubleshooting electrical problems, addressing software glitches or making on-the-fly adjustments to lighting cues as needed.

Both in rehearsals and the actual performances the lighting technician should maintain clear and open communication with the director, stage manager, and other members of the production team.

Lighting crew responsibilities

Skills required of a lighting designer:

- Creative vision for lighting design.
- Understanding of colour theory and mood setting.
- Technical knowledge of lighting equipment and techniques.
- Ability to create detailed lighting plans and cue sheets.
- Strong communication skills to collaborate with the director and other crew members.

Skills required of a lighting technician:

- Technical skills in setting up, operating and maintaining lighting equipment.
- Knowledge of different types of lights (e.g. spotlights, floodlights) and their uses.
- Ability to follow lighting plans and execute lighting cues during performances.
- Understanding of electrical safety procedures.
- Problem-solving skills for troubleshooting equipment issues.

Skills required of a lighting operator:

- Proficiency in programming and operating lighting consoles, or a willingness to learn.
- Ability to follow a script and execute lighting cues precisely.
- Quick reflexes and attention to detail to ensure timing accuracy.
- Communication skills to work closely with the stage manager and other crew members.

Sound engineer(s)

As with the lighting technician, the sound techie will usually be found within the student body but they will need the overall supervision of a suitably qualified adult. The sound engineer collaborates with the director and other members of the production team to develop a sound design that enhances the mood, atmosphere and storytelling of the play. This may include selecting appropriate music, sound effects and ambient sounds to accompany each scene or transition.

Sound technicians should assist with the set-up and installation of audio equipment, including microphones, speakers, amplifiers and soundboards. Again (health and safety), ensure that all equipment is properly connected, tested and functioning correctly before rehearsals and performances.

An important and often costly area is that of microphone management. If microphones are used, the sound technician will need to coordinate their placement and operation for actors, singers and other performers, to ensure clear and consistent sound reinforcement throughout the performance. This may involve using wireless or wired microphones, headset microphones, or lavalier microphones (lapel mikes), depending on the needs of the production.

During rehearsals and performances, the sound technician will programme and cue sound effects, music tracks and other audio elements using a soundboard or playback device. Create cues for each scene or transition in the play and synchronize them with the action on stage to enhance dramatic impact and timing. They should attend rehearsals to fine-tune the sound design, adjust microphone levels, and practise cueing sound effects and music transitions. They should work closely with the director and musical director, performers, and other members of the production team to ensure that the audio elements integrate seamlessly with the rest of the production.

Operate the soundboard or playback device during performances to execute the sound cues according to the timing and sequence established in rehearsals. Monitor audio levels, balance and clarity throughout the performance, making adjustments as needed to ensure optimal sound quality for the audience. (Once again, students should not have any drinks near the delicate sound equipment).

The sound technician must be prepared to troubleshoot any technical issues or malfunctions that arise with the audio equipment during rehearsals or performances. This may include troubleshooting microphone feedback, audio distortion, or playback errors to minimize disruptions to the show. Usually seated close to or next to the lighting technician, they must maintain clear and open communication with the director, stage manager and other members of the production team to ensure that the sound design supports the lighting and artistic vision of the play.

Sound crew responsibilities

Skills required of a sound designer:

- Creative skills in designing soundscapes and selecting appropriate music and sound effects.
- knowledge of sound equipment and software.
- Understanding of acoustics and how sound behaves in different spaces.
- Ability to create detailed sound plans and cue sheets.
- Strong communication skills to collaborate with the director and musical director and other crew members.

Skills required of a sound technician:

- Technical skills in setting up, operating and maintaining sound equipment.
- Knowledge of microphones, speakers and audio mixing consoles.
- Ability to follow sound plans and execute sound cues during performances.
- Understanding of sound safety procedures.
- Problem-solving skills for troubleshooting equipment issues.

Skills required of a sound operator:

- Proficiency in operating audio mixing consoles and other sound equipment.
- Ability to follow a script and execute sound cues precisely.
- Quick reflexes and attention to detail to ensure timing accuracy.
- Communication skills to work closely with the stage manager and other crew members.

Often, the lighting and sound engineer are the same person. When this happens, they will need helpers (crew) who will be responsible for the following.

Skills required for lighting and sound crew supervisor (staff):

- Leadership and management skills to oversee the lighting and sound crew.
- Strong technical knowledge of both lighting and sound systems.
- Excellent communication skills to coordinate with the director and other crew members.
- Problem-solving abilities to handle technical issues that arise during rehearsals and performances.
- Ability to create and manage schedules for the lighting and sound crew.

Skill required for assistant lighting and sound technician:

- Basic knowledge of both lighting and sound equipment and techniques.
- Willingness to assist with set-up, operation and maintenance of equipment.
- Ability to follow directions and support lead technicians.
- Strong organizational skills and attention to detail.

As these roles are sometimes split, but very often shared, I offer two experienced voices to cover all aspects of these vital roles.

Stuart Mantle

'I was never in a play myself, I was always backstage dressed in black. The school play introduced me to a world I was unaware of. It made me love people.'

Stuart is now an electrician, back then he was the guy who came to my aid on my first ever show. He continued to return to the school to help me light and mike a further five shows. During this time he 'passed on the keys to the cupboards', training the next generation of techies, who in turn trained the next and so it went on.

'The first show I watched was at the school I later attended. My cousin was in *The Greatest Show On Earth*. I was eight or nine and spent the whole time looking up into the rigs trying to work out how the magic happened. When I started at the school, no teachers understood or used the lighting equipment; an older student passed the knowledge down to the next willing boy or girl. You were the first teacher to show an interest.'

My top tips

'Directors, always listen to your technicians. Equipment has limits. Remember to cross-light and beware of shadows! Your techies need to know what your vision is so they can help make it a reality. Be open to suggestions. Making the space must be a collaboration. Avoid radio mikes! Understand what causes feedback! When recruiting the next generation of techies, look for the kid who's looking up!'

Favourite show I've been involved with

'My favourite show was *Bugsy Malone*; it was just sheer fun. The tech was the adult bit. Big and dramatic.'

Favourite show I've seen

'*Joseph and the Amazing Technicolor Dreamcoat* in 1998; it was the first time I'd seen all the new lighting effects and stages that started to hydraulically change live. No more curtains and flats. The whole stage just transformed in front of my eyes. Things that shouldn't light up did, without wires.'

Benjamin Hanlan

'Both my parents were drama teachers so I was always around during weekend rehearsals. I was drawn to the technical side. The buttons, lights and faders attracted me.'

Ben is an audiovisual production engineer at a fee-paying Catholic school. He has worked as a theatre technician in schools since 2016. He is also the son of this author.

'I did an apprenticeship in IT but the theatre was always on my radar. My first production was *Singing In The Rain*.'

My top tips

'I've always struggled with directors who can't describe their vison. They have to paint a picture and involve their team, including technicians, right from the start. Don't be afraid to come back to a director and communicate potential problems; if something isn't working, tell them. Do not be afraid of darkness on stage, don't over-light shows. However, always ensure there is some lighting backstage, blue blacks. Keep your space clean and free of clutter, I once had mice chew through the audio cable a week before a show! Don't buy cheap radio mikes, rent if you have to, they are better maintained and come with the necessary licensing. In technical rehearsals, be prepared to stop and start. It is not a normal run-through, it's for us, but it should also help the cast understand the importance of cues and stops.'

Favourite show I've been involved with

'My favourite shows to light have been *The Little Mermaid* and *The Addams Family*. I prefer simple sets with backdrop projections.'

Favourite show I've seen

'Oh, that's a tough one, Secret Cinema's *Stranger Things* was amazing, a fully interactive performance that you could walk through and interact with. It also had some amazing set pieces and tech absolutely everywhere, but blended really well.'

One more thing . . .

Shows can be diminished by singers shouting into microphones or performers standing in shadows! With this in mind, it is worth taking the time to teach your cast about the lighting onstage and how to use it to their advantage. Likewise, all performers using any type of microphone need to be taught how to get the best out of them!

15

Stage managing

I had this idea that I would sit in the auditorium and direct. This wasn't so difficult in the studio or classroom but once we started on the stage I realized things were happening that I couldn't see; things backstage and beyond my control. Shouting wasn't the answer, nor was running back and forth like some demented 'Jack of all trades'. What I needed was someone back there. Not just for ensuring cast and props were in place at the right time but that they were there at all! After a week of running around and barking instructions at unseen cast and crew, a fellow NQT from the English department saved my life and with calm efficiency became my saviour and the saviour of the show. She simply managed what went on back stage; she made it work. We called her 'the stage manager'.

In schools, this would more accurately be described as a 'backstage manager'. The role of stage manager is wider and in schools many of the responsibilities will fall upon the director. A student backstage team is vital to any show but the manager should be known to the students and have an authority in the school. The role is crucial for the seamless operation of everything that happens behind the scenes during a production. To me, a fundamental part of the role is to keep discipline backstage.

Warning: generally speaking, if the audience can see, hear or even suspect there's a backstage crew, something is wrong and some of the magic will be lost. You must have a stage manager. In the same way a musical director cannot be the pianist for rehearsals but should ideally conduct, so you, the director, have to be seeing what your audience will see. The stage manager is your eyes on what you cannot see. If your team is small and you simply don't have an adult backstage, the training of a highly responsible team of students will fall on you.

The stage manager is crucial. They ensure the production runs smoothly. Let's break that down into more manageable chunks with another handy list! It may well be that you will take on some of the following responsibilities, but in an ideal world your stage manager and their crew would take them on.

Pre-rehearsal/production

Organization and scheduling:

- With the director, create and maintain the rehearsal schedule.
- Coordinate with the director, cast and crew to schedule rehearsals, fittings and other activities.
- Prepare and distribute rehearsal scripts and schedules.

Script preparation:

- Make *prompt* copies of the script for cast and crew.
- Notate the script with blocking (stage movements) and cues.

Communication:

- Serve as the point of contact between the director, cast, crew and school administration.
- Organize and lead production meetings.

Resource management:

- Ensure all necessary materials and equipment are ready for rehearsals (props, costumes etc.).
- Assist in managing and tracking budget resources if applicable.

During rehearsals (the longest period)

Running rehearsals:

- Set up the rehearsal space.
- Keep track of rehearsal timings and ensure the schedule is followed.
- Record blocking and changes during rehearsals.

Communication:

- Address any questions or concerns from cast and crew.
- Relay director's notes and feedback to the cast and crew.

Problem-solving:

- Handle any issues or conflicts that arise during rehearsals.
- Coordinate with technical crew to address any technical problems.

Documentation:

Maintain detailed notes on the production process, including changes and decisions.

Technical rehearsals and performances

Coordination:

- Oversee technical rehearsals to ensure that lighting, sound and set changes are synchronized with the performance.
- Coordinate with stagehands and technical crew to ensure smooth transitions during performances.

Calling the show:

- 'Call' the show during performances; which means giving cues for lighting, sound and scene changes.
- Ensure all technical elements happen at the right time.

Backstage management:

- Supervise backstage operations, including managing props, costumes and actors' entrances and exits.
- Address any emergencies or issues that arise during performances.

Communication with cast and crew:

- Ensure the cast and crew are in place and ready before the show starts.
- Keep the director informed about any issues during performances.

Post-production

Wrap-up/strike:

- Coordinate with the crew to strike the set and return all rented or borrowed items.
- Ensure that the rehearsal space and any other used areas are cleaned and restored.

Feedback and evaluation:

- Conduct a post-production meeting to discuss what went well and what could be improved for future productions.
- Compile and distribute feedback to all involved parties.

Documentation and archiving:
Maintain records of the production for future reference, including scripts, notes, and any other relevant materials.

Helen Maree

'A moment of importance in their lives, no matter what they go on to do. During the production they grow in status and credibility.'

Helen is an English teacher and has been involved in stage managing plays in schools for thirty-four years. I have personally worked with Helen on five shows plus two Shakespeare festivals. She is also the very best stage manager I have ever worked with.

'My first experience of a school play was as a tree in *Wind in The Willows*. I first stage managed at uni for *Grimms Fairy Tales* and later, Equus. I would advise anyone thinking of volunteering to work as the school production's stage manager to simply do it! But follow these words of wisdom: you have to be super organized, you need to keep lists, don't be afraid to innovate and make suggestions to the director, be a strict timekeeper and, above all, don't try to do it on your own!'

My top tips

'I give everyone working backstage little blue gel torches. Strictly control access to the wings, keeping the bulk of the cast away until called. Line up props out of the way, not in the wings if possible. Get all props in place weeks in advance so that the cast can get used to them and where they will be. Drill it in to your crew with maps of where and when they and the props should be and why. Who takes it where and when. Nobody touches a prop or costume unless it's theirs or their responsibility. Be ruthless in protecting the performer who needs to know exactly where everything will be to within an inch. Recruit the students who want to be there, reliable is good but we can teach them that.'

Favourite production I've stage managed

'*Macbeth,* because it was visually powerful yet simple to manage.'

Favourite show I've seen

'*Phantom of the Opera.* I had never before seen anything on this scale theatrically or musically. Before I moved to the UK, my favourite show was a Theatre for Africa show (physical theatre) on the story of a young rhino whose parents were killed by poachers. Beautifully told with incredibly evocative movement.'

One more thing . . .

The stage manager is essentially the production's logistical hub, ensuring that every aspect of the show is organized, timely and smooth. If you get a good one, hang on to them, whatever it takes!

16

Costumes, make-up and hair

Wardrobe

You may be lucky, as I was in my first post, and have an almost magical person to help you with costume. Someone who knows the local charity shops, even volunteers in one of them. Someone who can make, adapt or source just about anything, from bridal gowns to a police uniform. A woman whose husband can turn his hand to making a coffin from plywood for Mr Sowerberry's funeral parlour. On top of that, she worked in the school, knew the students and really cared.

Joan was the ideal wardrobe technician, who could make, adapt, purchase, rent/source and repair. She was there from the start, but she wouldn't have said a word if I hadn't asked! If you don't have a Joan, where will you get character outfits, clothing for each character and those vital accessories such as hats and jewellery?

Students get very excited about the 'dressing up' part of drama and some will be very keen to assist in a school production. However, there is much more to the role than simply dressing characters. Costume design and selection, in collaboration with the director, help bring the characters, time period, and setting of the play to life. This process often involves researching historical costumes and sourcing or creating pieces that are able to seamlessly blend into the production's artistic vision.

At times, it will be all about finding that piece of costume and often there will be a need to make a piece from scratch or at least adapt an existing piece. Your school may have a costume box, bag, cupboard or a whole wardrobe department but at some point there will be a need to 'acquire, make or adapt' and some folk are simply 'experts' at knowing just where to go for that elusive tunic or dress, hat or pair of shoes. It may be from a professional costume hire company, or a search of the local charity shops or just knowing a school which did the same play a few years ago; but at some time, sooner or later, the person in charge of your wardrobe will need to be able to fix, patch mend and adapt. They will need to be able to sew! Quickly, expertly and sometimes in the dark! To be able to conduct fittings with the performers to ensure that the costumes fit properly and comfortably; and make any necessary alterations or adjustments to the costumes to achieve the desired fit and look for each actor.

With hired costumes comes the responsibility of maintenance and care, ensuring that the costumes are clean, well maintained and in good condition throughout the rehearsal process and performances. This may involve laundering or dry cleaning costumes as needed, maintenance and organizing storage.

They will need to be able to coordinate quick costume changes during performances to facilitate smooth transitions between scenes. This may involve assisting actors with changing in and out of costumes quickly and discreetly backstage. Wardrobe should also coordinate with the props/stage manager to ensure that costumes are accompanied by appropriate props and accessories as needed for each scene or character.

They will need to keep track of all costume pieces, accessories and related materials, maintaining an organized inventory to ensure that costumes are accounted for and easily accessible throughout the production process.

Creating a costume that works well onstage can be a very involved process. Here are some useful tips to ensure the costumes enhance and contribute to the overall production.

Research and understand a character's personality, background and motivations. A costume should reflect these aspects of a character, helping the performer inhabit their role more fully.

Do consider the physical demands of a performance. Costumes should allow performers to move freely and comfortably onstage. Avoid anything too tight, restrictive, or cumbersome that could impede movements or distract from the performance.

A costume should be visually striking enough to help define a character onstage. Therefore, pay attention to colour, texture and silhouette to create a memorable visual presence. Look to texture and colour to enhance a character's personality. Consider costume under stage lights.

If your production is set in a specific time period or location, the costumes should be historically accurate or stylistically appropriate. Research the fashion trends of the era to ensure your costumes suit the world of the play.

Think about practical aspects such as quick changes, durability and maintenance. A costume should be easy to put on and take off, especially if there are multiple costume changes during the show. Whether you have made, assembled or acquired a costume, you should ensure that it can withstand the rigors of performance without disintegrating!

Pay attention to the little details that enhance a costume, adding depth to a character. Think about accessories, props, hairstyles and make-up choices that complement the costumes and help tell each character's story.

A wardrobe technician will need a dedicated team to help with everything from acquisition and making to repair and fittings during performances. It is not always possible to put together the necessary team from students alone, and willing parents are often a very welcome addition.

Following is a handy list:

Costume acquisition and creation:

- Locate and source costumes: find appropriate costumes through costume hire companies, local charity shops, and other sources.
- Design and create costumes: make costumes from scratch or adapt existing ones to fit the needs of the production.
- Costume adaptation: modify costumes to achieve the desired look and fit, including alterations and repairs.

Fittings and adjustments:

- Conduct fittings: organize and conduct fittings with performers to ensure costumes fit properly and comfortably.
- Alter costumes: make necessary alterations to achieve the desired fit and look for each actor.
- Maintenance and care:
- Clean and maintain: ensure costumes are clean and well maintained, including laundering or dry cleaning as needed.
- Organize storage: manage and organize costume storage to keep costumes in good condition and easily accessible.

Costume changes during performances:

- Coordinate quick changes: facilitate smooth transitions between scenes with quick costume changes.
- Assist actors: help actors change in and out of costumes quickly and discreetly backstage.

Coordination with props and stage management:

- Coordinate with props/stage manager: ensure costumes are accompanied by the appropriate props and accessories for each scene.
- Manage costume-prop integration: work with the props/stage manager to ensure seamless integration of costumes and props.

Inventory management:

- Track costume pieces: keep an organized inventory of all costume pieces, accessories and related materials.
- Ensure accessibility: maintain an accessible system for costumes to ensure they are accounted for and easily found throughout the production process.

Character and performance considerations:

- Research character needs: understand each character's personality, background and motivations to ensure costumes reflect these aspects.
- Consider performance demands: design costumes that allow performers to move freely and comfortably onstage.
- Enhance visual presence: pay attention to colour, texture and silhouette to create visually striking costumes that define characters onstage.
- Ensure historical accuracy: for period pieces, ensure costumes are historically accurate or stylistically appropriate.
- Plan for practical aspects: ensure costumes are durable, easy to put on and take off, and can withstand the rigors of performance.

Attention to detail:

Add final touches: enhance costumes with appropriate accessories, props, hairstyles and make-up choices that complement the character and production.

Health and safety:

See risk assessments in Appendix G.

After the show:

- Inventory and collection: ensure everything is accounted for and in good condition/repair.
- Returns: any items borrowed or rented should be cleaned and returned
- Storage: all items to be kept should be repaired/cleaned and stored safely and suitably.

Joan Wilcox

'I can't act, sing or dance but what I can do is enable students to act, sing and dance on stage and look their best in a costume I provide.'

Joan was a learning support assistant for ten years, and she also worked as our wardrobe mistress. I worked with Joan on ten school shows and a further two in a second school, where she gave her time to students who were not her own. Such is the generosity of the woman. To be honest, the idea of putting on a show in my new school without her was too much for me, so I unashamedly poached her.

'As a child I would help my mother who was an apprenticed seamstress. I believe no student should be disadvantaged in a school production because they don't have the correct costume or are unable to provide one. I aimed to build up a core of costumes for the school to be self-sufficient because the hire of costumes is too much for a small drama budget.'

Top tips

'You will need patience. Working with all age groups, some of them very young, in an environment which is very different from their normal school day.

Try to find like-minded people to help with skills or time, this includes pupils who want to help, find a task for them, exclude no one. Enjoy the challenges.

Make sure you understand the director's vision.

Every student thinks their costume is the most important, remember it is to them.

Keep lists of each character, actor name and the costume items required for each scene – list every item, including footwear! Label each piece of costume with character, actor name and scene.

Safety pins – you never know when there might be a wardrobe malfunction!

Do not refuse help from a student, not all young people want to be on the stage but might wish to be a part of the production.'

Favourite production I've costumed

'I cannot say which was my favourite show. I loved working on all of them.'

Favourite show I've seen

'I still remember my first Shakespeare, *Othello;* it was a school trip in my fifth form, that was a great experience. It was so wonderful to see the words being spoken instead of reading them in class.'

Make-up

Stage make-up is not everyday cosmetic make-up. Stage make-up enhances the actor's appearance on stage, making their features visible and expressive to the audience. If you decide your performers require make-up, it should be purchased as a personal consumable product. There are many online companies specializing in stage make-up.

Make-up, much like costumes, is a highly popular element of the school play among students. If your school offers courses in beauty therapy, wellbeing, hairdressing or related fields, you'll find plenty of students eager to contribute their creative skills to the production.

As with all areas of a school production, there should always be a suitably qualified adult in overall charge.

The role of the make-up artist during a school play will be to enhance the appearance of actors and bring their characters to life through make-up techniques. Their key responsibilities would include collaborating with the director and costume designer to understand the vision for each character and how make-up can contribute to their portrayal on stage through the development of make-up designs that reflect the personalities, emotions and characteristics of selected characters in the play. This may involve researching historical or thematic make-up styles and techniques that are appropriate for the production.

Members of the team would be required to apply make-up to actors before performances to transform their appearance into the characters they are portraying. This could include applying foundation, concealer, powder, blush, eyeshadow, eyeliner, mascara, lipstick and other make-up products to achieve the desired look for each character. If required, students could study and create special-effects make-up, such as wounds, scars, ageing effects or fantasy creature designs, to enhance the visual storytelling of the play. This may involve using prosthetics, latex, wax or other materials to create realistic or theatrical effects on the actors' faces and bodies.

Under supervision, the team could provide guidance and advice to the performers on skincare, make-up application techniques and maintaining their appearance throughout the final rehearsals and performances.

Members of the team would be need to be available backstage during performances to provide touch-ups and adjustments to actors' make-up as needed, ensuring that they look their best throughout the show.

During the process, the team should be available to assist performers with removing their make-up, using gentle and effective techniques to ensure that their skin remains healthy and undamaged by following the correct hygiene practices and using sanitary tools and products to prevent the spread of germs and bacteria during make-up application and removal.

Collaboration and design:

- Collaborate with director and costume designer: work with the director and costume designer to understand the vision for each character and how make-up can enhance their portrayal.
- Develop make-up designs: create make-up designs that reflect the personalities, emotions and characteristics of each character. This may involve researching historical or thematic styles and techniques.

Make-up application:

- Apply make-up: transform actors' appearances using foundation, concealer, powder, blush, eyeshadow, eyeliner, mascara, lipstick and other products to achieve the desired look.

- Special-effects make-up: create special effects such as wounds, scars, ageing effects or fantasy designs using prosthetics, latex, wax or other materials to enhance visual storytelling.

Guidance and advice:

Advise on skincare and techniques: provide guidance on skincare and make-up application techniques to performers, ensuring they maintain their appearance throughout rehearsals and performances.

Performance support:

Backstage touch-ups: be available backstage during performances to touch up and adjust actors' make-up as needed, ensuring they look their best throughout the show.

Make-up removal:

Assist with make-up removal: help performers remove make-up gently and effectively, ensuring their skin remains healthy and undamaged.

Hygiene and safety:

Follow hygiene practices: use sanitary tools and products to prevent the spread of germs and bacteria during make-up application and removal. See risk assessments in Appendix G.

Supervision and guidance:

Students should work under the supervision of a suitably qualified adult who is in overall charge of the make-up department.

Warning: the make-up team will be responsible for ensuring that the actors' skin is properly prepped, allergy tested and cared for before make-up application to minimize the risk of skin irritation or allergic reactions. Hair and wig stylists (if required) should work closely with the make-up and costume teams.

Norma Cockroft

'The school play matters. It shows everyone that anything is possible.'

Norma has been head of hair and beauty and a special educational needs coordinator (SENCO) for eleven years. She has been involved with school plays for the last twenty years.

'When I was fourteen, I appeared in a 'mods and rockers' version of the *Pied Piper*. I was a mod, and the make-up and hair were an important part of the show and stuck in my mind.'

My top tips

'You need to be really organized, it's not a salon. Time is important. Know the director's vision for the show, the characters. Research the era and look at film/photos of previous productions. One student per main character (subject) with organized character specific packs each. They should get to know their subject and consult with them over their make-up requirements and any allergies etc. Teach your subject how to remove their stage make-up. Always read your labels! Practise under pressure (timed).'

Favourite show I've been involved in

'*Bugsy Malone,* 1920's New York and Gangsters!! For costume and hair it's wonderful.'

Favourite show I've seen

'My favourite stage show was *Matilda,* I loved how the lyrics had a sharp, clever wit about them. Also the choreography was so energetic and sharp. I particularly enjoyed the iconic Miss Trunchbull and the way she commanded the stage; an unforgettable experience.'

One more thing . . .

Over the years, I have become a bit of a minimalist; however, if a script demands specific costumes and make-up, I have a simple set of guidelines. They should enhance and never detract, be safe and not inhibit the performer, whilst suiting the period and character.

17

Your cast and their parents

At the tender age of 13, I was abruptly uprooted from my quiet, charming secondary school nestled atop a steep hill in the valleys of South Wales, and placed in a bustling, sprawling, noisy school in the flat concrete suburbs of Surrey, England. The contrast was stark, I was an alien in an alien land.

The harsh tarmac of the playground, the endless corridors swarming with teachers and bullies; all of them eager to pick on the new boy with the strange name and Welsh accent. Every break and lunchtime became an exercise in survival as I tried to escape my 'new friends,' who never had anything kind to say or do to me. I took refuge wherever I could: in the shadows, the library, even the chess club! I drifted among the other misfits, seeking some kind of sanctuary.

Then, one lunchtime, I stumbled upon the drama club: a warm, safe and non-judgmental space, mercifully windowless. There, I joined in improvisation games and harmless distractions. Sometimes, I even enjoyed myself. A little. But soon, the teacher who ran the club asked me to step out of hiding and perform in front of the whole school. I wanted nothing more than to stay invisible; but he insisted, eager to 'get me involved'. I thought it was another of life's cruel jokes, but he was sincere – and passionate about drama. So, I went from being a lunchtime refugee to being part of something.

My first experience with a school play was backstage, where I could hide in the shadows and watch, unobserved. I was safe, unseen and – finally – unbullied. But there was something else; there in that kind, enveloping obscurity, I discovered the transformative power of the theatre. I fell in love with the whole wonderful process. 'The school play!' It was *Charley's Aunt* by Brandon Thomas. The audiences roared with laughter for three performances in a row and I realized right from the opening night that I wanted to be out there, under the lights, making people laugh, cry, reflect and go home different. The next year we performed a play written by the drama teacher to a packed hall of proud parents and pals.

Being part of the school play changed me. It gave me much-needed confidence and a real sense of achievement; but I also felt like I belonged to something special, something different. I believe the school play discovered me rather than the other way around. I wonder how many drama teachers, actors, directors, technicians had their first experience of the theatre on the school stage, involved in a school play!

Your cast

You see your cast five days a week. Many of them are your students; they are in the classes you teach. They call you Sir, Miss, Mrs, Ma'am or Mister and occasionally, in a moment of unguarded familiarity, even 'mum' or 'dad.' You know them, and they know you; but how well do you truly know them? Directing them is different. When it comes to directing, understanding your students goes beyond their names or faces. You need to know their skills; what can they really do? How much of themselves, and how much commitment will they bring to the project? This deeper understanding of your cast can make all the difference in guiding them to success on stage. Make auditions a place where they can show you something extra, something you may not have been expecting and maybe has nothing to do with the text, but that you can add to the play.

There's the acrobat, the ballet or street dancer, singer, musician, amateur magician, parkour runner, martial arts student, juggler, tightrope artist, or those with another language, sign language or mime. Then there's the artists, carpenters, costume designers and makers, sound people, lighting people, DJs; they all have transferable skills. Sometimes, the comfort students feel when using their own expertise in an audition enables them to overcome nerves and become bolder artist. The mantle of the expert!

Your students are imaginative, creative, artistic, emotional, empathetic, generous, agile, adaptable and multi-talented. Sometimes, they simply don't tell us! We must enable them to bring all their talents to the process of making art, so make it optional that they can also demonstrate a skill at audition if they so wish. I allow a space for this on the audition form (Appendix A), but it's up to you.

Chanel Waddock

'I was always trying to find my tribe. I saw the school production of *Grease* in my first year at secondary school and I was hooked.'

Chanel is a working actor/artist whose television work includes: *The Outlaws, London Kills* and *This Is Going To Hurt*. Her stage work includes *Chariots of Fire, Bitter Lemons* and Frantic Assembly's production of *Othello*.

Chanel was a student of mine, who appeared in several shows and always gave that extra sparkle.

'Why was I hooked as a year-seven, watching *Grease*? The camaraderie. Walking around school day to day and seeing the members of the cast from different year groups socializing. It totally shattered the idea of hierarchy for me as a fresh-faced member of the school. These people were daring and I wanted to be part of it.'

'My first school production was *Oliver!* I was one of the boys, but I was part of a community, a shared experience. So many people all committed to the same force! At first, it was all about the bow and the applause, but I learned it was really about the story. Not only the playwright's, but our story as a company. One drama teacher's motto was: "It's not the destination, it's the journey". Call it a cliché, but it fostered the best philosophy for young creatives making art. It allowed the art to evolve and for new discoveries as performers. It made us present! A key component when wanting your students to create their best work; it invited us to lose our inhibitions and feel freedom in our work.'

Advice to a new teacher/director

'In auditions, get people up and acting, playing and inventing. You asked us to try and pick-pocket you for *Oliver!* You had silk hankies hanging from your pockets and we had the chance to offer ourselves, our ideas, we loved it. Offer a space for students to be authentic in their expression – authenticity is the aim! For rehearsing? Go for a positive experience. Lots of energy. Boost morale, gratitude and encouragement. I guess this ties in to everything but the most important ingredient I think is trust! Trust which is made within the room from both director and cast, which is infectious within a cast. I'm going back to what had me hooked; seeing people chatting in the canteen at lunch, exchanging birthday cards in corridors and chucking a smile across the playground. It's infectious and so fantastic! And afterwards, when a show is over there is a sense of loss, almost grieving, look after your students after the final curtain falls.'

Favourite school production I was a part of

'My favourite school play was *Hamlet*, I played Gertrude and loved the dark and the ugly. Later, I went on to play Laertes at the National.'

Favourite show I've seen

'*Yerma* at The Young Vic.'

Parents

Parents are vital! I have worked with many wonderful, generous and talented parents over the years. Some are hands-on and roll their sleeves up, painting, sawing, sewing and glueing. Others are the shuttle service who deliver their children/your cast and crew, to and from rehearsals beyond school hours and over weekends. They make sandwich, tea and soft drink drops, ferry other cast members around, drop off bits and pieces and keep the whole thing going. Most of all, they support their children, deal with the tired, irritable and insecure; the tantrums and the egos. But above all, they tell their children that they can do it, and by doing this they support you.

Involving parents not only helps in the logistics and execution of the show but also builds a supportive community around the performance, enriching the experience for everyone involved. And, of course, they buy lots of tickets!

Heather Pugsley

'Many parents are so willing to help. But ask us, or we will assume you only want us as taxi drivers!'

Heather is a parent of two highly successful students, one of whom appeared in many school shows and went on to study drama at Bristol Old Vic.

'My parents were Salvation Army Officers, so from an early age I saw the value of being able to speak in public and even sing! When my son became involved in school productions I was happy to help out. I enjoyed being part of the show, not just driving my son to and from rehearsals but being asked to help. So, apart from the driving and bringing snacks and drinks, I made the headdresses for the fairies in *A Midsummer Night's Dream* because I was involved and asked! During school shows, my son was always happily focussed; this stemmed from being part of close group with a shared experience.'

My top tips

'Communicate with the parents about everything. Honour the schedule, insist they wear comfortable clothes, especially for weekend rehearsals and that they have snacks and drinks on hand. Keep them hydrated! As a parent, I want the students to look as professional as they can be on stage. I want the lighting, sound, costume and scenery to help them shine.'

Favourite show I've helped out with

'*A Midsummer Night's Dream*, because I was involved, I was a part of it.'

Favourite show I've seen

'*Les Misérables*. The music and the love!'

Alethea Truin

'When we didn't have shows, the school was diminished.'

Alethea was a parent governor at the school where I first taught drama. She had two sons at the school and both were in a number of my productions.

'For my sons, being a part of a school production meant self-esteem, they learned the importance of timekeeping and empathy but above all, they made friends and memories.'

My top tips

'If you're having trouble convincing senior management, ask them what they remember of school? Do they remember their school productions? Everyone needs to be able to speak in public. The school show gives young people a chance to shine, it builds in resilience, teaches them about life's disappointments as well as its highs. Make sure the caretaker and staff are on board.'

Favourite school production

'*A Midsummer Night's Dream*, everyone shone!'

Favourite show I've seen

'Would be *Henry V*, but I also have a soft spot for Pinter's *The Caretaker*.'

18

Timescales, lists and schedules

I once put on a school show whose final weekend dress rehearsal and opening night clashed with the final weeks of the World Cup. Result: missing students from vital rehearsals and virtually no audience on two nights. I heard a lot of, 'Surely you knew?' and 'What were you thinking?' None of which was very helpful. But I did learn a couple of important lessons. Always check well in advance and don't mess with the national sport, even if England hadn't qualified for the final. Well, I wasn't teaching in 1966!

This chapter looks at planning the right time, not just for the performances, but the rehearsal season; looking at potential clashes with the school's academic calendar and beyond. School productions are extracurricular. This chapter covers how to ensure a fair/even spread of time slots which do not become a burden to students or staff whilst remaining sufficient for a great show. The actual rehearsal process is covered in depth in Chapter 21, 'Rehearsing'.

When I sit down to plan a schedule, I have a large-scale calendar in front of me and begin with potential performance dates (production weeks) and work my way back to the present with each one. Next, I check on possible clashes and major events like holidays/exams etc. and blank them out in red! At this point, I make a decision on the dates with the least potential clashes. Still working backwards, I then put in my weekend run-throughs, tech and dress rehearsals. I then calculate how much time my cast/crew and I will need. How many hours a week and which days. This varies depending on the play; for example a large musical production will need more time than a conventional piece of drama. The more parts, the more time etc.

The total amount of rehearsal time needed for a school drama production can vary significantly based on many factors, including the complexity of the play, the experience and maturity of the students, and the frequency of rehearsals. However, a general guideline for planning a well-rehearsed production should go as follows.

Auditioning and casting: time frame: two to three weeks.
Once you have selected your play and studied it you should give at least two weeks to holding auditions and casting the roles.

Initial read-through: time frame: one week.
A read-through of the script with the whole cast to discuss characters, development, themes, and other production elements.

Blocking rehearsals: time frame: two to three weeks.
This is the precise staging of actors in each scene and is a critical phase where the physical movements and positioning of actors are determined.

Scene work: time frame: three to four weeks.
The detailed work on individual scenes to refine acting, pace and delivery. Scenes can be broken down into smaller parts for intensive work.

Run-throughs: time frame: two to three weeks.
Full or half run-throughs of the play, working on continuity, transitions and the pace of the piece.

Technical rehearsals: time frame: one to two weeks.
Bringing together lighting, sound, costumes, props and set changes. Tech rehearsals are critical for integrating all production elements.

Dress rehearsals: time frame: one week.
Full costume and make-up rehearsals, typically with minimal or no interruptions, to reflect real performance conditions.

This gives a minimum total rehearsal time of eleven weeks and a maximum of sixteen.

I run my rehearsals three to four days a week, with each session lasting two to three hours. As the performance dates get nearer, more frequent or longer rehearsals will be needed, particularly during the final two to three weeks. I do five days a week during the final two weeks.

This approximate time frame is a good indication of the level of commitment required by cast and crew and I always include a summary of it in the audition information pack (see Appendix A).

Remember to build some flexibility into the schedule to account for unexpected issues. Consider the academic and extracurricular commitments of the students. This increases as they move further up through the school. Include short breaks during rehearsals to maintain focus and energy, thereby ensuring students have adequate time to learn their lines, develop their characters, and get comfortable with all of the technical aspects of the production. Adjustments can be made based on the needs and constraints of your school and the production, but try to stick to schedules as much as possible.

Planning and communication

Availability: survey the availability and other commitments of students and staff. Talk to the exams officer, the head of PE for sports fixtures, other bookings of the venue etc. Use this information to create a schedule that accommodates the majority.

With all the information/dates at hand, plan your rehearsal schedule well in advance, ideally before the school year starts or at the beginning of the term. Communicate the schedule to everyone concerned (students, parents, and staff) as early as possible, using printed copies and using communication platforms such as email newsletters, parent-teacher apps, or social media channels. I always put a copy in the staffroom.

Consistent time slots: rehearsal time slots should be consistent to help students and staff plan their other activities around rehearsals. For example, set rehearsals for 3:30 pm to 5:30 pm on specific days of the week; e.g. Monday, Wednesday and Friday.

Weekly commitment: limit rehearsals to two to three days a week initially, increasing to four to five days as the performance dates approach. Aim to make rehearsals shorter at the beginning and extend them closer to the performance dates.

Lunchtimes: lunchtime rehearsals are often impractical, with many schools having short lunches. You and your cast need to eat and relax! However, there have been times when I've needed to call in one or two for a brief piece of choreography or vocal/instrumental work.

Balanced schedule: schedule rehearsals on non-consecutive day, this gives students time to rest and focus on academia. Avoid scheduling rehearsals on consecutive days until closer to the production dates.

Weekends: use weekends sparingly! I use a maximum of two. Ensure any weekend rehearsals are included in the schedules from the start and not 'added as needed'.

Stagger your rehearsals: after the initial read-through, try to begin with smaller group rehearsals focusing on specific scenes, before progressing to full-cast rehearsals. In this way, you minimize the time each student needs to be present, initially.

Prioritized rehearsals: try to prioritize scenes with more lines or complex choreography early in the schedule. Leave simpler scenes for later rehearsals. But don't under-rehearse them! This is another reason to have an in-depth knowledge of the play and its requirements.

Set clear objectives: have clear goals for each rehearsal to ensure productive use of time. Share these goals with students so they come prepared and focused.

Supporting the staff: having surveyed their availability, other commitments etc., sympathetically delegate responsibilities among the staff who have generously volunteered to be a part of the production; such as stage management, technical direction, and costume supervision. Rotate staff involvement to avoid burnout.

Supporting the students: if needed, encourage students to support each other through peer rehearsals or study groups for line learning. Set up a WhatsApp or similar group for cast/crew members to share schedules and news. (Remember to check school social media policies.) Hold regular check-ins with students to gather feedback and make necessary adjustments. Be flexible and willing to adapt the schedule as needed based on feedback. Monitor to ensure no student or staff member is overwhelmed by their workload and stress levels.

A typical rehearsal schedule

Weeks one to six

- Monday, Wednesday: 3:30 pm–5:00 pm and Friday: 3:30 pm–5:00 pm.

Weeks seven to ten

- Monday, Wednesday, Friday: 3:30 pm–5:30 pm.
- One weekend rehearsal (Saturday or Sunday): 10:00 am–2:00 pm.

Weeks eleven to twelve

- Monday, Tuesday, Wednesday, Thursday: 3:30 pm–6:00 pm.
- One weekend rehearsal: 10:00 am–5:00 pm (Saturday and Sunday).
- Saturday full technical.
- Sunday full dress.

This is followed by the production week. I have a full dress/tech run through on the Monday or Tuesday, then I usually set three performances; one on a Thursday, Friday and Saturday evening at 7:30 pm with a twenty-minute interval for large productions. For younger students, try to start earlier so that they can finish in good time, especially on a school night. Smaller shows and studio performances can fit in and around other school schedules and may be a one-off. I avoid doing two shows in one day. Remember these are not professional actors and have full school lives to consider.

By planning thoughtfully and maintaining open communication, you can create a rehearsal schedule that balances the demands of the production with the other responsibilities and well-being of students and staff. Remember, not all cast will be needed at all rehearsals. Be sure to give them a break, even the principals.

Top tips

- Book any spaces well in advance. You may think the studio is yours, but are there any external clubs who rent the space?
- Develop a rehearsal schedule that accommodates the availability of your team members, taking into account school commitments, extracurricular activities and other obligations.
- Be flexible and considerate when scheduling rehearsals, and communicate any changes well in advance.

One more thing . . .

Stick to times. If you tell parents and students a rehearsal will end at 6:00 pm then ensure it does. Keeping those willing parents who taxi your cast back and forth waiting is not a good idea!

19

Auditions and casting

I place a high value on inclusivity and diversity in theatre, recognizing its power to amplify marginalized voices and promote social justice. By casting a wide range of actors, embracing diverse perspectives and challenging stereotypes, we can build an artistic community where everyone feels seen and valued. Yet, when casting a production, it's essential to consider each actor's readiness and ability, ensuring they can thrive on stage. While I encourage all students to audition, I also take care to protect them from vulnerability or insecurity, which can arise when actors aren't fully suited to a role or lack insight into their character. Ultimately, my goal is to foster a passion for theatre that goes beyond performance. School productions should be a space for personal growth; building confidence, empathy, and a lifelong appreciation for the arts.

As drama teachers, we are constantly seeking ways to raise the profile of our subject. A school play is a great start, but really it's about raising the profile of the whole school. The school play is not a recruiting tool for your subject, you do that in other ways. I have worked with great performers in schools, who have taken part in every production but have not chosen drama as a subject. I have also had drama students in my senior classes who have wanted no part of the school production. We should not be surprised by this nor try to force students to 'change their minds' or to not 'waste their talents'. The school play should transcend such notions, only then can it be truly inclusive.

There are different types/methods of auditioning students. Sometimes it all depends on the type of production; for example, a musical will require singers and often dancers, too. But it also depends on your students, some audition well in the traditional sense, others will need other opportunities to demonstrate their talents.

Before auditions commence

Announce the next school show with as much pomp and ceremony as you deem appropriate. Build a tradition of this. Hold a (well-advertised) meeting for anyone interested, where you describe the show. Describe the show/brief plot outline if they are not familiar with it already. Give dates, both for any weekend rehearsals and the performance night(s). I always invite a member of the senior team/head to this introductory meeting, along with a cordial invitation to all staff, including non-teaching. Whole school is whole school. Remember, you will need your site manager/caretaker/janitor onside.

You should talk about the expectations and commitment required for the production. Set a professional theatre tone. Tell them about weekly after school/lunchtime rehearsals and the importance of punctually attending all that they are called for. As they leave, those interested will take an audition information pack with them (Appendix A). The pack will contain audition dates, times and all information needed for an applicant for acting and non-acting roles (tech/front of house), including tips/guidance on how to audition well. I include audition materials/script sections. I furnish students with audition materials to ensure equal opportunities for all. If they select their own, it puts them under pressure to find appropriate materials when you already have them at your disposal. Their choice may not adequately demonstrate the talents you are looking for. If you are looking for a specific performance, you should be specific with the material you provide. This applies to lines, lyrics, and dance routines. Be aware that some students may have problems accessing written materials; this should not exclude them.) This is why I call auditions at least two weeks after the initial meeting where the audition information packs are handed out. During this time, students can access recorded versions of the texts if they need them. The pack also includes a form to be signed by the student, parent/carer and form/class teacher.

There are many different ways of running an audition and different styles suit different schools/colleges and your students. I personally run them with a fairly professional tone, as I often have a great number of students applying. The process should run as smoothly as possible, which means giving clear guidance/instructions right from the start. Students should know what they are applying for, where and when the audition will be and how they will need to prepare. There will always be the students who need extra encouragement to take the risk of auditioning, so individual auditions help but remember they will need to perform in public if they get cast.

At this point, I feel I should give one of my **Warnings!** You may have ideas about who you would like to play a specific role, indeed you may have decided that now is the time to mount this production because you have students of a particular type/skill set in your classes. However, and this is important: NEVER tell a student you are thinking of them for a specific role or suggest they apply for a specific part. Rather, encourage all students to consider applying and once they have read the information pack (Appendix A) make a decision based on their own preferences. They should be encouraged to discuss their choices but do not be tempted to hint at promised parts. This is for the following reasons: it's unfair, unprofessional and you don't know who else might turn up and give a perfect audition! Students are very likely to notice any favouritism, and will be uncomfortable with it. Auditions often result in a degree of disappointment; it's the nature of the business and managing it is an important lesson; there is no need, therefore, to increase the potential for disenchantment, jealousy or resentment. Such things can fester and have no place in a show.

The auditions should be called for at least two weeks after the initial meeting. All applicants should bring their signed form to the audition. No form, no audition (this also applies to potential crew). Collect them and keep them (They are important!)

Some teachers don't use auditions at all, preferring to select students from their drama classes. I strongly urge against this even in the smallest school. This is a school play. Theatre classes can have their own intimate studio performances to showcase their talents. The whole-school production must be just that. But that is my personal opinion.

Running the auditions

I begin all auditions with a whole-group workshop-style warm-up, where everyone is included, even the non-acting students. During this first session, I explain how the audition process will work. Next, we move to group readings from the script. During this session, you can mix and match students to get an idea of strengths before auditions for specific roles later, with smaller groups. The individual auditions do not take place in this session. In this first workshop I am looking for team players as well as talent. Try to create a positive and inclusive atmosphere for all students.

Within a day or two, I start the individual or paired auditions. Paired auditions are useful as a way of students supporting each other in what can be a nerve-wracking time.

Tips for running auditions

1. Schedule individual slots and try to keep to these timings.
2. Ensure there is another member of staff or adult to supervise a waiting room close to the audition space.
3. If possible, try to ensure you have an assistant with you as well as any musical/dance specialists needed for each audition.
4. Create a welcoming atmosphere by preparing the audition space. Ensure it is private, quiet and comfortable. Greet each student warmly. Auditions should be a fun and positive experience for everyone involved. Keep the atmosphere light-hearted and encourage students to enjoy the process.

5. Clearly explain what they should expect during the audition, including any prompts or directions you may give them. Answer any questions they may have before they begin.
6. Encourage relaxation by offering simple techniques, such as deep breathing or visualization, to help students calm their nerves before they start their audition.
7. Encourage them to be creative and interpret the material in their own way rather than trying to mimic someone else's performance.
8. Offer support and encouragement: throughout the audition, offer words of encouragement and support to help students feel confident and valued. Remind them that auditions are not just about getting a part but also about learning and growing as performers.
9. Be attentive and engaged, paying close attention to each student's performance. Engage with them by maintaining eye contact and nodding or smiling in encouragement.
10. Allow for multiple takes: if a student makes a mistake or wants to try a different approach, allow them to start over or try again. This can help them feel more comfortable and confident in their audition.
11. During the audition, I take notes. At times they are hastily scribbled in a way I can't decipher later. Some like to keep a score system where marks are given, say out of ten. But I'm a scribbled notes person. I have a number of criteria: How prepared/professional is the student? How well do they understand/articulate the character and needs of the piece? Their use of pace, pitch, pause and projection; do they fit the vision you have for the piece or lead you to consider another direction? Be sure to keep all of your notes secure and private, ready to refer to when casting.
12. After each audition, offer constructive feedback to help students improve. Focus on the positive aspects of their performance as well as areas where they can grow.
13. At some point in an audition, I give students the chance to show a skill they have which may be nothing to do with the show, but could very well be! Students often surprise us with the things they keep quiet about. (See Chapter 17, 'Your cast and their parents'.)
14. End on a positive note: thank each student for auditioning and let them know when they can expect to hear back about casting decisions. Ending on a positive note can leave students feeling encouraged and appreciated.
15. It is important to maintain professionalism during auditions. Treat each student with respect and courtesy, regardless of their performance. Respect confidentiality: keep students' audition performances confidential and avoid discussing them with others outside of the audition process.

Callbacks

I try to avoid callbacks and the added tension they cause, not least of all for the students. Any I do call, I do in pairs or more. I make sure I know exactly what it is I am trying to resolve/look for and design a seemingly informal improv workshop rather than get them revisiting their initial audition piece. I am looking for specifics like: What is the most challenging aspect of their character's performance? Their onstage chemistry; how do they look and perform together? Acting and reacting; their generosity as a performer; What they give to the piece.

And so, to casting . . .

Casting

I try to put a preliminary cast list together as soon as possible. I then consider it for a few days; what my father used to call 'sleeping on it'. Only I don't sleep! I always find this the most difficult part of the process. Occasionally, the play almost casts itself and it's all obvious and easy. But more often than not, it's a jigsaw that just refuses to fit! Above all, remember your notes and keep emotions out of it. Knowing the play intimately is vital, as is keeping your artistic vision firmly in sight.

Keep an open mind. Be open to unexpected interpretations and talents. Students are full of surprises and may force you to reconsider pre-conceived casting notions. Despite always wanting to have a professional overview of the whole process, we have to bear in mind we are educationalists first and foremost. I try to accommodate as many of my students as possible in the 'whole-school production'. However, I have a golden rule of never putting a student on stage who doesn't want or deserve to be there. If a student is uncomfortable or embarrassed on stage, they shouldn't be there. I will add extras to a scene to allow stage time for those who deserve to be there but will not shy away from refusing others.

Consider the ensemble: while you're looking for individuals who shine, also consider how each student will fit into the overall ensemble. Look for chemistry between performers and consider how different personalities will complement each other on stage. Trust yourself and your professionalism!

Consider cross-gender casting. Often (in mixed schools), there will be more girls auditioning than boys. If you have an imbalance of boys or girls, it is not a bad idea to consider cross-gender casting. Likewise, if you are short on suitable cast, multi-role is a creative solution that works well. I once had a very strong female cast, but was very low on boys, We were doing *Romeo and Juliet*. I had no Lord Capulet, but a very strong Lady Capulet so removed him from the story and gave his strong brutal lines to Lady Capulet. It really worked as Shakespeare in particular allows for such creative solutions. What I don't usually do is ask a girl to play the part of a boy or vice versa. Strictly speaking (where possible) you should obtain permission from the playwright before making any changes to their script.

Does the show have specific race requirements? **Warning**: colourblind casting is one thing, but certain shows such as *Hairspray*, *Othello* and *Miss Saigon* have specific racial requirements that must be honoured, or else it will affect the piece. For example, *Othello* cannot be played by a white male. Aim for an inclusive and culturally mixed cast, which reflects the make-up of your school and community.

Taking risks: there have been occasions when I have offered a role to a child who has behavioural issues in lessons. Taking a leap of faith and giving your trust to these pupils can result in a huge boost to their self-esteem. However – and I'm going to be controversial here – such students have to display something that will benefit the ensemble and the play. I do not believe the play is the place for behavioural problems to be sorted out. This is not a therapy session; too many students, staff and parents will have put so much effort and emotion into it.

You know your students best, and if there are any uncertainties, their tutor or parents can provide additional insights. Consider students who would benefit from participating in the show, but also assess the potential impact on the entire production.

Based on past experience, it is generally advisable to approach casting with caution regarding students who have significant attendance issues, as this can affect rehearsal consistency. For guidance, please refer to the tutor's/homeroom teacher's signature and comments in the audition information pack (Appendix A).

This consideration goes beyond behaviour alone; it reflects respect for the dedication of the entire cast. Please also consider whether the student's commitment to coursework or exams might be at risk, as frequent detentions or exclusions could affect their ability to keep up with the demands of both the show and their academic responsibilities.

Students with disabilities in school productions

Including students with disabilities in school productions is a powerful way to break down barriers, challenge stereotypes and foster a more empathetic and connected community. I have had the privilege of working with deaf and hard-of-hearing students, as well as students with mobility impairments. For instance, a student with cerebral palsy thrived in the role of Oliver, while others who use mobility aids have excelled as cast and crew members. What they all shared was a strong desire to be part of the production and the capability to contribute meaningfully.

Thoughtful inclusivity ensures that all students feel comfortable and supported in their roles. Every student should have the opportunity to showcase their talents in a way that aligns with their abilities and interests, making the production stronger and more enriching for everyone involved.

It's important to recognize that all students – regardless of ability – are key stakeholders in the production. They are the ones learning lines, developing characters, and bringing the story to life for their peers and families. Their commitment and contributions are invaluable and deserve recognition and respect.

Letting them know!

Once you have agreed upon your cast, how do you post it? Some post it on a general noticeboard in the school or a dedicated drama noticeboard. Others do not favour this for, whilst it celebrates the success of some, it also makes public the disappointment/rejection of others. I would take you back to the point I made about teaching students to deal with disappointment and rejection, but it really is a matter for serious consideration.

Another method is to call everyone back and announce the cast. This again is public but at least it's limited to those who were interested and not the whole school population. It also gives you the opportunity to praise everyone and perhaps comment on difficult decisions.

The third method is to individually, usually by written word/email, contact every applicant and inform them of the decisions/casting. This gives students the opportunity to react privately before informing friends and family in their own way, in their own time. Bear in mind though, that at some point a printed cast list will have to be made public.

However you announce your final cast, it is always good practice to list them alphabetically by character and not by importance of role. I have always favoured the posting of a cast list on the drama noticeboard. It fits in with my ethos of making the school play as professional and 'real-life' as possible. I aim to post on a Friday afternoon on the drama noticeboard. This way, students have the weekend to process any feelings of disappointment, euphoria or rage. I accept that this is not for every school. I would not, for example, use this method with primary/elementary school students; in this case, I would favour a group announcement with only those who auditioned present. With the posting of the list, I retire to my office/studio. Students know I'm there and, although I will not give feedback there and then, I will be around if students are particularly upset. It isn't easy but the promised feedback sessions the following week help.

Helping students deal with rejection

When I was at school, I considered myself a funny kind of kid. I could make people laugh, I had timing and any number of voices. I auditioned well, I thought, for the part of Sir Toby in *Twelfth Night*. When I didn't get the part, despite learning the lines (all of them), my first reaction was one of disbelief, followed by anger, which later settled in to a belief that I was simply rubbish at everything. The feedback I received was 'better luck next time', which didn't really help. My mum told me to try for a smaller role next time, and maybe she was right. I felt rejected and unimportant for a while, but luckily I was not deterred. I'm sure others were.

At some point, we have to face the fact that not everyone will get a part. Some will be disappointed and have real feelings of rejection. My older students, in particular those who have chosen to study theatre as a subject, will be more able to deal with rejection. But younger students, in particular those for whom this is their first foray into the theatre can become despondent and tearful. Rejection is tough to deal with and dealing with it publicly is not pleasant for younger students. Built in to that first meeting must be the warning that not everyone will get a part or the part they wanted. I feel that this should also be included in the audition information pack (Appendix A). Students who know they worked hard and feel they auditioned well will feel the rejection keenly and can react with feelings of anger and self-doubt. For this reason, feedback at audition should be gentle and complimentary, yet honest. Yes, it's even difficult to put in a sentence! A school production is not all fun and this part is tough for students, but it's tough on the teacher too.

Forewarning and discussions about not getting the part you wanted (or any part) are vital. I try to use current, relevant and classic examples in this part of the process. For example, I love Danny DeVito and he was great as Matilda's father, but I wouldn't cast him as Romeo. Or Robert Pattinson as Batman in *The Batman* (2022). Pattinson's casting brought a fresh intensity to Batman. However, casting him as Thor in the Marvel series would be entirely different, as he does not align with the character's specific style and persona.

Such examples can help students understand that even talented actors may be suited to some roles but not others, and that casting involves matching the right actor with the character's needs.

I offer audition feedback sessions for everyone who went for a part. These routinely take place a week to ten days after the audition. Students who choose to attend their feedback session find that the time elapsed has given them space to gather their thoughts and hopefully lose some of that raw emotion. Everyone is made aware of these sessions right from the start. They are referred to in the audition information pack. The process can be time-consuming, but it is vital for everyone regardless of the outcome of their audition because they offer the following.

- **A constructive learning opportunity**: feedback provides insight into strengths and areas for improvement, helping all students grow as performers. This guidance can reinforce positive choices they made or highlight adjustments they could work on in future auditions.
- **Encouragement for future efforts**: for students who didn't get their desired role or any role at all, feedback can soften the disappointment by showing them that their efforts were recognized.

Constructive feedback encourages resilience and signals that their potential is valued, motivating them to keep developing their skills.
- **Transparency and trust**: feedback creates transparency in the casting process, building trust between students and the director. It reassures students that casting decisions are thoughtful and purposeful, rather than arbitrary, fostering a sense of fairness.
- **Celebrating the successful auditions**: for students who did receive roles, feedback highlights what they did well, building confidence and helping them understand why they were cast. This can also provide them with specific directions to enhance their portrayal of the character.
- **Community and support**: group feedback sessions (if you choose to do it this way) can foster a supportive environment, showing that everyone is working toward a shared goal. Students can learn from each other's feedback, which helps them understand different approaches and styles, and deepens respect for one another's talents.
- **Preparation for future auditions**: giving feedback, especially to those who may not yet have the technical skills or experience of others, provides a roadmap for improvement. It prepares students not only for school shows, but also for other performance opportunities by helping them develop professional skills for auditions and accepting feedback.

One more thing . . .

Giving feedback is part of what we do as teachers; indeed, it should be part of the school's culture/ethos. Students expect nothing less.

20

The first cast and crew meeting

'Oh sir, by the way, I won't be here for the dress rehearsals at the weekend, I've got a football match.'

'Mum says to tell you my sister and I can't make the final performance as we are going on holiday.'

'If I'd known I would have changed it, honestly.'

'I can't rehearse after school, I'm not allowed.'

'I have lunchtime revision classes all month.'

'I was in detention again.'

'Oh, that was today?'

'Sorry I'm late.'

'Sorry!'

Take your pick, you will hear some if not all of these during a production run, if you haven't already!

I will never forget my Bugsy Malone going away on holiday Saturday morning with a show looming the following week. His parents got last-minute tickets, 'They were a bargain sir, we couldn't say no, could we?' Or my Tybalt being permanently excluded and Inspector Goole being conflicted over rehearsals and football practice. There is very little you can do and it's not about that. It has to be about how you avoid it ever happening. This is the main purpose of that important first cast and crew meeting.

Your own drama students know you, they are aware of your expectations, but not all who audition are so well trained or so well intentioned!

Note: before you have a meeting for cast and crew, get together with your adult team and go over roles and responsibilities first. This is a good time to advise and help any NQT/ECT to manage their time.

The first meeting for cast and crew

All of your staff/adult team should attend the first cast and crew meeting, as this is where they will be introduced and their roles explained to the students.

At this first meeting, you should address the vital issues like attendance, so insist everyone turns up! There can be no exceptions, as this one sets the tone. First, it is important to congratulate everyone present as successful in becoming part of a team. This is going to be extraordinary, memorable and magical; but it will also be challenging and at times tough!

Everyone involved will get an overview of the story and what it will look like (the vision); and an overview of the roles and responsibilities and how to manage the demands on their time. Other commitments, clubs, homework/exams, getting home late, possibly in the dark: you must cover it all at this first meeting. Reiterate the importance of communication with home and school over rehearsals, and communicate with parents about the commitment their child is making, ensuring copies of the rehearsal schedules are sent home, received and understood. Before they go, you should announce date/time and venue for the 'cast read-through', which should take place soon after this meeting. They should also be given their personal copy of the rehearsal schedule agreement form/contract (Appendix F), which they should complete at home and bring back to the read through.

You might consider setting up a general WhatsApp group for all cast and crew as an electronic version of the noticeboard. **Warning:** I do not use my personal number for this and you should check on school policies concerning sharing contact details.

A checklist for that first cast and crew meeting

Attendance
Confirm that all cast and crew members are present (take a physical register).
Emphasize that attendance is mandatory and crucial for setting expectations.
Highlight that missing meetings/rehearsals affects the entire team.

Congratulations and team spirit
Celebrate everyone's successful audition or application.
Stress the importance of teamwork and supporting each other.

Overview of the story and vision (the show pack)
Introduce the show pack and refer to it throughout the meeting.
Provide a clear summary of the story.
Describe the overall vision, themes, mood and style of the production.
Ensure everyone understands and aligns with the creative direction.

Roles and responsibilities
Outline each person's role and responsibilities.
Discuss balancing these roles with other commitments.
Address any potential challenges related to travel, time management or other commitments.

Introduction to theatre etiquette
Set ground rules for punctuality, respect, and professionalism.

Explain the importance of following directions from directors and stage managers.

Building confidence and addressing uncertainties
Address any nerves or uncertainties about roles.
Provide encouragement and support, and clearly explain each role's contribution to the production's success.

Setting expectations for rehearsals and performances
Outline the rehearsal schedule and discuss the importance of attendance.
Set clear behaviour expectations on and off stage.

Communication
Stress the importance of communicating with home and school about rehearsals.
Ensure that parents are informed about their child's commitment and rehearsal schedules.
Distribute, receive and confirm understanding of rehearsal schedules.

Rehearsal schedule agreement form/contract (Appendix F)
This form should be handed out at the end of the meeting.

Encouraging creativity
Inspire participants to explore their creativity.
Encourage contributions of unique talents and ideas to the production.

Questions and clarifications
Allow time for questions and clarifications from the cast and crew.
Outline any follow-up actions or additional meetings that may be necessary before the schedule begins.

Ensure everyone leaves with their copy of the show pack (see below).

The show pack

Each student involved will receive a show pack. Cast and crew have different packs (Appendix B).

Schedules and dates

This will include dates, rehearsal schedules.

Synopsis and history

I also include a synopsis of the play and any historical notes.

A who's who guide; who the adults involved are and an explanation of their roles.

Rules and contracts

A list of expectations. The pack includes a contract. It's always a good move to get the students to help you put together a contract, but you will need to set aside time for this. Include what they expect of one another etc., why this is important and then what happens if they don't (sanctions). As we know, students are more accepting and understanding of rules they have helped put together.

Rehearsal guidance

Include in the pack Appendix E, 'The Student guide to successful rehearsing'.

Language of the theatre

See Chapter 22 and Appendix C.

Rehearsal schedule agreement form/contract

See Appendix F.

One more thing . . .

If you are new to the school, get a more experienced colleague, perhaps your mentor, to look over the show pack to ensure it conforms with the school/college's regulations and values.

21

Rehearsing

'Sir, this is boring!'

That idea you had about a highly choreographed piece of physical theatre to introduce the scene just isn't working. You've spent over an hour on it. Everyone hates it and they probably hate you too right now. They're tired, bored and mutinous, and it's your fault.

And there it is again: 'Sir, do we have to?' and, twenty minutes earlier, the answer should have been 'No! No we don't'. It should have been, 'Let's leave it for now' or 'Let's try something different!'

The school play isn't a lesson or a class; it's extracurricular, voluntary and different; a time when students become actors, singers, dancers and technicians. You become a director, a producer and perhaps the choreographer to boot, but you will also remain the teacher at all times, which can be a difficult balance.

Rehearsals are filled with highs and lows. Those moments when everything clicks, and then the deflating ones when the cast and the whole show seem to be slipping through your fingers. It's a journey; you have to be flexible and adapt yet at the same time set the example and stick to your schedule. You can't give in to the temptation of blaming the cast and shouting at them. Students should leave rehearsals feeling positive, and yet! The well-placed 'Director's tantrum' should be avoided at all costs. I allow myself one per show, but it must be purposeful and never personal. Remember, these are young people giving up their time because they share a vision with you. So, one tantrum if you really need to, but no blame.

The greatest lesson I've learned over years of directing students is to never waste time. That's both your time and theirs. Don't have the two protagonists rehearse their three special lines whilst the rest of the cast sit and fidget. Don't let time run away with you; if you say twenty minutes to run through a scene, then that's it, twenty minutes. Rehearsals will take up as much time as you give them, so be wary when putting your schedule together (see Chapter 18, 'Timescales and schedules').

Guidance for directing a rehearsal

Be punctual and set the example by arriving promptly for all rehearsals. This establishes a professional environment and ensures that everyone benefits fully from each session.

Plan ahead by creating a detailed rehearsal schedule, including deadlines for learning lines, blocking, and technical run-throughs. Share this with your cast and crew early on (see Chapter 12).

Have a clear vision and stick to it. Keep it on paper and refer to it often.

Know the script thoroughly by reading and understanding every scene, character and theme, ensuring you know how they fit with your vision.

Do a read-through: it's not everyone's cup of tea – some like to get stuck straight in – but I find a whole-cast read-through with tech and crew present is of great value. It can be a fun and bonding experience, leading to a greater understanding of the text as well as a prompt for valuable questions and answers (as long as you don't continually interrupt, no matter how tempting!)

Set clear goals for each rehearsal; have specific objectives, whether it's working on a particular scene, developing character relationships, or running through a section without stopping. Your cast should be aware of these goals before they start the rehearsal.

Warm-ups should be done at the start of each rehearsal. Combine physical and vocal exercises. These help students to relax, focus and get into character.

Focus on blocking by establishing the movement and positioning of actors on stage early in the rehearsal process. Try not to continually change things. I know it's tempting as a piece develops, but it can confuse students, which in turn leads to a loss confidence.

Develop characters by encouraging students to think deeply about their characters' motivations, backgrounds and relationships. Use exercises and discussions to help them bring these elements to life.

Incorporate technical elements gradually by introducing aspects like lighting, sound and set changes over a period of time. This will help everyone get used to the full production without becoming overwhelmed.

Encourage collaboration from the start, by involving students in the creative process. Encourage them to share ideas and work together on problem-solving. This will make them feel more invested in the production.

Avoid overlong rehearsals, which can get boring. Avoid leaving students standing around waiting whilst others go over a scene/section without them. It's difficult, but try to get everyone engaged for most of the time. This is where an assistant (older student) can be very useful. Plan for short breaks (but with clear limits as to where they can go and for how long).

Never overrun in a rehearsal, no matter how desperate you are. I have been one of those patient parents who sit in their cars waiting for their child to stagger out into the daylight. Don't use up that patience and goodwill; it's vital you retain parental support.

Create a positive vibe by fostering a supportive and encouraging atmosphere. Praise effort and progress, and address mistakes constructively.

Keep it varied. From time to time, I will introduce – as appropriate – a basic acting technique lesson. It helps with focus and the feeling that 'everything is for a purpose'.

It is also good to bear in mind that constantly going over and over the same thing doesn't always make it better, sometimes it just makes it boring. Be prepared to drop an idea, ask the cast to try ideas or another member of staff to try a fresh look at the scene. But stay positive; 'I give up, you got any ideas?' is not what we're talking about here.

Use student assistants. If you have a student assistant director, use them and listen to their ideas.

Wrap-up. Make time for a notes-giving session where you gather everyone for constructive feedback (cast and crew). Highlight the strengths and areas for improvement, emphasize the importance of continuing to work on lines and character development. Encourage the cast to practise their lines and blocking at home. Always end by reminding everyone of the next rehearsal and any specific tasks they need to focus on. End on a positive; if you have time do something together, play a game to warm down.

Be flexible and prepared to adjust your plans based on how rehearsals are progressing. If something isn't working, don't be afraid to try a different approach. Don't over-rehearse or flog that dead horse.

Guidance for students

Your students will need guidance too. Appendix E contains a suggested list of expectations/requirements of students for a successful rehearsal entitled; 'The student guide to successful rehearsing'.

Note: the crew get their own guide too.

Helping students learn their lines

Learning all of those lines can be a problem for many performers and equally difficult to address in a short space of time.

A cast member who finds it challenging to learn lines will soon hold up rehearsals and be limited by not being script-free. However, let's face it, some find learning lines difficult, while some find it easy. As teachers, we know our students learn in different ways and we have to find which suits them best, just as we would in the classroom. After the read-through, I give a workshop on line-learning. I make it fun and non-threatening; a game, not a test. I begin with some memory games and then ask them how many songs they know the lyrics to. I follow this with, 'and why do you know those words so well?' Their answers are often the key to their learning style. It could be repetition, association, the tune, a rhythm or rhyme and even the way they move to it. Let them think about this for a while; it's often a revelation to them.

Then introduce them to the many methods they can try. Here are my tried and tested preferences, you probably have some of your own too.

Repetition

Reading and repeating. The much-favoured method of reading the lines several times in chunks and having a friend or family member test them with cues.

Writing it down

Write out the lines by hand, onto a sheet of paper; with notes and diagrams if that helps. Then try writing them from memory. This can be done on phones or laptops/tablets if they prefer. Some students who share scenes like to text their lines/dialogues back and forth to each other or use group chats to help in the process.

Post-its

Some surround themselves with post-it notes and stick them all around their house. Try using different colours for different scenes or changes in mood.

Auditory learners

A very successful method goes back to hearing that favourite song over and over. I get the performers from a scene together with scripts (read-through style) and record, perhaps simply on their phones, the text they need to learn. They send the recording to each other and listen to it on their headphones as often as they need. Many students say this is the method which makes a difference for them. I recommend listening to the recording one final time before they go to sleep at night. Some students prefer to make their own recordings just for themselves on their phones but I point out that unless they have large monologues/soliloquies, it's always better as a shared experience, as they need to hear their cues. It's always better as a team effort. An extension of this is to just record your cues and try to fill in the gaps. Some like to record only their cues and learn their lines from that point.

Visual learners

Visual learners love to sketch a form of comic strip/storyboard of their scene cues and lines. Visual learning can include:

- Mnemonics: some students will be familiar with this method and will have used it successfully in their academic studies. They create acronyms, phrases or visual images to remember lines.
- Mind mapping: where students create a visual map of the script, connecting different parts of the dialogue with visual cues or symbols.
- Mime and shadow practice: the method of simply mouthing the words or performing the lines silently to internalize the rhythm and flow without vocal strain.

Kinaesthetic learners

Kinaesthetic learners (I'm one) find it great to walk the talk. I walk, move, even dance my way through dialogues and monologues, associating an action with a line whilst listening on my headphones. It looks crazy to an onlooker but, for me it's the best and it's all about finding which method or combination of methods work best.

Contextual learning

This is closely associated with the kinaesthetic approach, where understanding the character's motivations and emotions, knowing why a character says a line can make it easier visualize and associate it to movement.

Partner work

This is where students pair up with another student or a friend to practise lines. Which is great for getting the feel of the back-and-forth of a real performance.

Using apps and technology

Many students will want to try apps designed for script-reading and memorization. There are several line-learning apps and digital flashcards out there.

One more thing . . .

No matter how people learn, everyone should break down the script into chunks/scenes and not try to work through large, overwhelming pieces in one go. Encourage your students to try a mixture of these methods and experiment to find what works best for them!

22

The language of the theatre

The school play should be an immersive, group collaboration in which the entire team of performers, designers, makers and technicians all feel they are making something special. I always try to foster a very close bond between the whole team. Seeing the shy year-seven child acknowledged by senior performing arts students in the corridor, because they know him as the lad who helps backstage always reminds me that a family of artists is being founded and friendships that transcend age or levels of coolness are being made. A sense of belonging to something special develops and is tangible throughout the school. Bonds are built between students and staff alike. They are having a shared experience which will stay with them; an experience which will shape and educate them.

Whilst sharing time together, as well as an artistic vision and all the ups and downs of a production, it is important to share a sense of professionalism. This includes the professional performer, the technician, the stage hand; the whole team. With this in mind, and as part of the learning process, I introduce everyone involved to many of the technical terms most used in the industry. This avoids confusion such as 'No, I mean your left, not mine' or 'Pull the rope thingy next to the wooden bit with the wheels!' Students like the professional feel and just knowing something different. Just as the director must communicate their vision clearly to cast and crew including technicians and designers, the actors also need to express their needs, ideas and concerns using the same terminology. Familiarity with technical terms helps ensure that everyone is aligned and can work together effectively. So, as a part of the information pack, I include a glossary of technical and theatrical terms they will be hearing over the next few months (see Appendix C).

Understanding the technical language of theatre is like a musician mastering their scales: it's the foundation of the craft. It's vital for the entire team; just as a director needs to communicate their vision clearly to actors, technicians, and designers, actors also need to express their ideas, needs, and concerns using the same shared language. Familiarity with technical terms ensures that everyone is aligned and able to collaborate smoothly. Theatre is live, and unexpected issues can arise. By knowing the technical language, your team will be better equipped to troubleshoot problems during rehearsals or performances. Whether it's adjusting lighting cues, managing sound levels, or handling set changes, this knowledge empowers everyone to find solutions quickly and without confusion.

There are many highly technical and specialized terms used in the business, but we don't need to overwhelm or fry our brains with all of them. Appendix C is an alphabetic list of the terms you and your cast/crew should be familiar with, with notes on regional differences. I include this list as part of the show pack which I give every member of the team right at the first full meeting for cast and crew as part of their show pack.

Understanding the technical vocabulary of theatre isn't just about speaking the same language – it's about unlocking a richer understanding of how the magic happens onstage. As students look into these terms, they'll find that they're not just tools for communication but gateways to a deeper appreciation of the intricate artistry behind the production. They will hear them used regularly in rehearsals by you (the director) and the technical crews.

One more thing . . .

Just like teachers of foreign languages should use the target language in the classroom, the director should never be heard to say, 'Stand over there next to the thingy'.

23

A collection of minor disasters

. . . and what to do about them!

It was opening night and the curtain call on *Romeo and Juliet* was in less than an hour, when a panic-stricken stage crew broke the news, 'Sir, Juliet is unconscious!' I rushed in to the classroom set aside as a green room and, sure enough, Juliet was lying on the floor with two members of staff tending to her. Apparently, in an excited pre-show adolescent show of cast madness, Tybalt had – with Juliet upon his shoulders – raced Romeo – with Lady Capulet as his rider – up and down the corridor. Romeo, being shorter than Tybalt, had managed to avoid crashing his mother-in-law-to-be into a the top of a door frame; sadly, Juliet was not so lucky. Her real parents were called and, as they were parking in the carpark at the time, they arrived on the scene fairly quickly, just as their daughter was coming around. They took some convincing, mainly by their daughter, but she did go on to perform that evening. What was equally alarming was how the panic spread and other normally sensible cast members began to cry, feel faint and generally over-react! Being so hyped up and full of pre-show adrenalin, everyone, it seemed, was about to have a panic attack! It took me sitting them all on the floor and doing breathing exercises to get the cast down from the ceiling. The moral of the story? Your cast need calm adult supervision pre-show, and with absolutely no 'horse play!'

So, what can go wrong?

Here are a few more personal experiences.

I've always had one golden rule for any actor wearing a radio mike: never touch it. There's a whole team of tech wizards backstage for that. They'll mike you up, switch you on, and control everything from their sound desk. Easy, right? Well, that was the plan . . . until the sound tech was about five seconds too slow. The lead actor dashes off stage left, believing he's safely out of earshot, and loudly confesses to his partner, 'I just f***'d up my song!' Of course, his mike was still very much live. So now, not only does his partner know, but so do the audience, his mum, dad, gran, and of course the head teacher. It doesn't just happen to politicians!

Or there was the unforgettable moment in our production of *Oliver!*, where a certain Dickensian villain was supposed to be shot while dramatically escaping over the rooftops of London. The starting pistol, which should've fired blanks, didn't fire at all! Cue a moment of awkward silence as poor Bill, ever the professional, decided to mime his own death. With great flair, he clutched his heart, staggered dramatically, and threw himself backwards onto the crash mat six inches below. Then, just to add to the magic, as he hit the ground, a very helpful – though slightly late – member of the stage crew shouted, 'Bang!' Yeah, that totally sold it!

Timing is everything!

Then there's the perfect timing on our second night of *Hairspray*, just as Tracy Turnblad sang the line 'I can hear the bells', and our fire alarm went off. Her composure as she improvised with 'Yes, I really can' and led the cast off stage, was perfect. After fifteen minutes in the staff carpark, we returned, complete with the audience and restarted the show.

Whether it's during a performance or just days before your opening night, there are some things you cannot plan for; some things just happen and it's all about how you and your cast recover.

I have survived illness and injury close to the performance date, stage fright, lost lines, an opening night and World Cup final clash, Blousey Brown being permanently excluded one week before the opening night, technical problems from a broken plug to burned out lighting desk, feedback so bad our ears almost bled, the wrong splurge gun backfiring and a fiddler being sick on the roof.

Remember, an audience will forgive most things. 'This is the theatre, they will believe us!'

The school audience in particular already loves the cast; they come with invested emotions and a willingness to believe. That's part of the magic. However, here is my list of the top ten things that can diminish that magic. Avoid them whenever possible!

1. **Warning:** 'Shh' is more audible to an audience than the excited low murmur of backstage crew and cast! A well-meaning stage manager's attempts to quieten any backstage chatter with prolonged 'shushing' is a real atmosphere killer unless the scene is actually featuring *Thomas the Tank Engine!*
2. Overlong, complex scene changes. Keep scene changes simple and fast or in the interval. Always look for the least disruption to the flow of the play (the magic).
3. Poor sightlines. This could mean sections of the audience not having a good view or that some of them can see backstage. During dress

rehearsals, I move around the auditorium seating to check different sightlines and perspectives of the stage.
4. Slow and missed lighting cues. Don't leave your audience or performers in the dark!
5. Feedback and/or microphones cutting in and out. Clothes rustling with poorly fitted lapel mikes.
6. Moving set and flats. Ensure everything is fixed securely in place.
7. Costume/hair/make-up that are inappropriate for the time/theme.
8. Unintentionally comical or poorly thought-out props.
9. Vocal ranges not suited to singers.
10. Timing! Timing is everything. Entrances and exits, lines and sound cues. It's not that they're being mean, but audiences do laugh at poor timing and when you don't want it, laughter is cruel.

Trouble with your audience!

Yes, audiences are not without blame either! But how do you reduce their often well-meaning disruption without causing offence? There is nothing quite as upsetting as a performance spoiled by its audience. This can take many forms, all of which are equally frustrating for a cast and crew who have worked tirelessly to give their very best.

Top of the list comes the dreaded mobile phone! Apart from the light of the screen being a distraction for cast and other audience members, ringing phones and even conversations such as, 'I'm at the school. What? Can you hear that? Yes, it's a musical!' And it doesn't stop at phone calls, photographs and even videos of performances are also within the skill set of the smart phone.

It upsets and embarrasses performers when their mum or dad, aunt or uncle are so thoughtless. So what can you do? Notices in the programme, signs on the walls. An announcement at the start of the show. It's still almost guaranteed someone will either forget or believe no one will call them during the show. I have made announcements at the start of shows asking that the students hard work be recognized by everyone now switching off their mobile devices. I have gone on to (partially lie) and claim mobile phone signals interfere with radio mikes and sound equipment, and still some folk think it doesn't apply to them. I know I'm ranting here and not providing solutions. Short of confiscation (which I don't think we can get away with), all we are left with is making it very obvious that only a really terrible person would leave their phone on during the show, let alone play Candy Crush during the performance. One way of deterring the phone photographers is to offer a time at the end of the show when cast will be available in costume for photographs. I don't like doing this as it extends the performance and feels a little unprofessional, but it can help.

Then there are the sweet rustlers! Well, we can start by not selling crisps and other noisily wrapped edibles in the concession shop. Yes, it can raise extra revenue but perhaps sell them in soft plastic bags. I leave up signs saying 'Strictly NO eating in the auditorium'. It's meant for the students during the day, but if the cap fits!

Costumes/props and/or set designs that are mismatched with the theme or period of the production can break the illusion of the performance and make it harder for the audience to suspend their disbelief. Careful research and consultation at the early stages helps eliminate this. Look at stills/videos of professional productions of the same show.

Technical glitches that persist throughout the performance, such as constant feedback or lighting cues being missed, can create a sense of unprofessionalism and detract from the overall enjoyment of the show. Double-check everything and ensure cables are well fitted and covered. Remember, a way to minimize such things is to incorporate the technical elements into rehearsals as soon as possible.

Planning helps and, as a part of this, you should carry out a thorough risk assessment! (See Appendix G.)

There will always be challenges along the way, but with solid preparation and professionalism, your show is bound to be the success it deserves to be.

One more thing . . .

To help balance out those rare but daunting scenarios, here are my top ten tips to ensure your production is nothing short of spectacular:

1. Passionate, well-prepared performances where the cast connect emotionally with their roles.
2. Clear, creative vision and strong direction.
3. A well-crafted, dynamic set. Imaginative simplicity can be just as effective as elaborate designs.
4. Effective lighting which enhances the mood, emphasizes key moments and helps focus the audience's attention.
5. Creative costumes that reflect characters' personalities and the play's era/setting. Good costumes also enable students to connect with their roles.
6. Engaging music and sound effects. Well-timed sound effects or atmospheric background music can elevate the emotion of a scene and enhance audience engagement.
7. Pace! Keep the energy of the show high by ensuring smooth transitions between scenes and maintaining a rhythm that doesn't drag or feel rushed.

8. Diction and projection. Make sure your students project their voices and articulate clearly so the audience can hear and understand intentions.
9. Polished movement. For musicals or plays with significant movement, well-rehearsed choreography adds that professionalism and excitement to the performance.
10. Audience engagement/interaction. If appropriate for the production, finding ways to engage or interact with the audience will create a memorable experience that leaves a lasting impact.

24

How it played out

School productions are always memorable in their own unique way. Over the years, I've been involved in many, often stepping into the roles of director, producer, set builder and painter. These shows are fuelled by dedication, long hours and the kind of teamwork that creates truly unforgettable experiences. Here are some moments that have stayed with me.

A Midsummer Night's Dream

I love this play for its high fantastical, magical, enchanting escapism. It makes us laugh and giggle like small children whilst all the while recognizing the course of true love weaving its way amid the laughter. It works on many levels and with all ages. I wanted to put it on more than any other Shakespeare I ever studied. So I did, three times so far.

Having used the mechanicals many times to get young students engaged with Shakespeare, I was always delighted to have students who wanted to play the various characters. They brought so much to the parts. I'm a massive fan, but something I've always found with Shakespeare is that no matter how well you think you know his works, actors always bring something new to the stage. A different perspective, a new meaning, or a subtle change of pace. Such was the man's understanding of the actor.

My first production of *The Dream* was very early on in my teaching career. I wanted to move away from 'end-on' staging, instead going for a traverse stage, with the audience sitting on three sides of what was essentially a thrust, but at audience level. At one end, I had the stage where the elevated action of Athens took place and then the whole of the wide thrust was the forest (where the magic took place). I used most of the length of the main hall and had the audience four rows deep at each side and five deep at the end. I wanted the forest area to be littered with foliage, leaves and small twigs etc. What I didn't want was painted trees as props dotted around the performance space blocking sight lines everywhere. This is a problem when you perform in what is, essentially, 'the round'.

One dress rehearsal, the caretaker saw what he called 'rubbish' all over his nicely polished floor and made it very clear this would not be happening. After a few hours of panic, I came up with the crafty solution of using a vast canvas tarpaulin spread over the majority of the forest performance space. I rented it from a specialist tarpaulin supplier who kindly donated it to the school in exchange for an ad in our programme. When it arrived, it was large, dirty, paint-spattered and smelly. But it worked. Perfectly. So the day before the opening night, I sent the whole cast out to the school field, which was skirted by various large trees, to bring back foliage for our first performance. We laid it all out on the tarpaulin and it was very pleasing. Just after the students left for home, the caretaker came in to lock up and to reminded me that there would be an assembly in the hall first thing in the morning and that I'd better get this mess cleared up! He had a point. So my stage manager and I rolled the tarp – complete with all the leaves and twigs – right back to the stage, where it sat like the large roll of dirty, damp, leaf-filled tarpaulin it was. It was then that I had one of those last-minute ideas that put a cast on edge. We would now have a slight change to the stage management and get the mechanicals at the end of Act One, Scene Two to roll out the tarpaulin to reveal the forest floor. We practised it once about an hour before the audience came in! Which is when I had the second idea, to roll it back up at the end of Act four, scene two; back into that large sausage-like bulk in front of the stage, where it would act as a vast decadent cushion for the dukes, lords and attendants to watch the performance of Pyramus and Thisbe on the main stage. The cast were fantastic and fell in with their daft director's last-minute changes. It could have been a disaster! But it worked beautifully and with an added wonder, which took us all by surprise. The damp leaves and snapped pine twigs had spent a night rolled up in a tarpaulin, and then the whole of the first act under stage lights in a crowded hall. When Peter Quince and his crew unrolled the tarpaulin to reveal the forest floor, the smell of the forest was very real and transported our audience to a magical woodland better than any green gels, projections and sound effects. In the local paper, they even gave special mention to the 'highly creative' idea of making the performance space even smell like a forest. Sometimes it just works like that.

Although I went on to direct *The Dream* twice more, I never used the leafy tarp again. Every time is different. Different cast, different venue, different feel. I used live music to great effect in my second production with the mechanicals playing djembe drums. It gave them a real power and pace throughout the performance.

I've been an audience member in a promenade performance which walked us through a local woodland and was privileged enough to see it performed in Central Park, but my greatest memory will always be that opening night when the smell of damp, warm pines filled our school hall.

Bugsy Malone

Bugsy is a firm favourite. Everyone loves the bad guys, the dames and the double-crosses; but most of all, we love the splurge. It's one of those shows the students ask, nay beg, you to direct. It had been on recently in a school not too far away, so we left it for a year, which only made the excitement grow and when it came time for auditions, it was standing-room only! Even ex-students asked if they could be in it!

So it's a great show, an all-time favourite and hit with students and audiences alike. But it should come with some splurge-related warnings! The first thing about *Bugsy* is it's well known, it will sell out; but before that can happen, you will spend a lot of your budget on the ready-to-hire costumes and splurge guns out there, not to mention re-fill cans of the legendary white foam! Indeed, adverts abounded on how and where to hire the all-important guns, but one look at the costs and we decided we had the technology to design and make our own. How hard could it be? As it turned out, very hard indeed. But our design guys and their students made it a project. Our splurge guns looked the part, they felt right and even made a noise. But when we fitted the cans of splurge, it all went horribly wrong. The project had taken months, with each test spraying more expensive splurge everywhere but out of the barrel of the gun! The pipe was too thick, too thin, the trigger was too loose, the barrel was too heavy and fell off! Of the six guns, one is scripted to backfire. Well, they kind of all did that, or just poured the expensive foam out of the side. In the end, I took an executive decision and used God's gift to the theatre: gaffer tape (duct tape), and simply taped a can to the side of the gun's wooden butt and the actors just sprayed as scripted. It worked and everyone was happy, well almost everyone.

Some notes on splurge (avalanche spray/custard pie foam)

- Ensure your cans of splurge are non-toxic and come with COSHH/OSHA safety certificate.
- Generally, shows get through one 400 ml can of splurge, per splurge gun, per show.
- Cans usually spray about 3 metres, depending on the temperature.
- Look online and you will find a number of suppliers in your area/country. Some even specialize in props for *Bugsy Malone*. Shop around, they can be expensive.
- A tip from my experience would be to rehearse with half-used cans by all means, but always start a performance with new cans.

Warning: note for the wardrobe department: take care with hired costumes, get them into warm water as soon as you can after each show. Or wipe them down (suits). Splurge will come out, but has been known to stain, especially in dark fabrics if left overnight. Hand wash in lukewarm water.

During our one full splurge rehearsal, we came upon another little problem they didn't tell us about and we hadn't considered! After eight cans of splurge, a stage begins to not only look like a snow-covered ice rink, it also acts like one. Funny, but dangerous. We thought of crews coming out and wiping away the offending splurge during scene changes, and the character Fizzy was used to come on after a fight and mop the stage while remaining in character, but this didn't help during the actual splurging scene. So, out came the old faithful tarpaulin and the stage was made safe, but not before a few bruising encounters!

Too much splurge (is there such a thing?) will make a wooden stage surface slippery and, as it dries, sticky and horrible underfoot if not cleaned again with warm water after each rehearsal and performance.

Grease

I had this great idea: let's go to a local scrap yard and get a real car. We will advertise them in our programme and they will 'give' us an old wreck. They did, they even delivered it to the school one Saturday lunchtime and left it square in the middle of the staff carpark. The staff were really impressed! The tech department offered to perform the necessary surgery to make it safe and suitable for the stage. They sensibly emptied the tank, removed the oil and any other dangerous components and we pushed the lightened remains into the main hall, where we encountered problem number one. Removing the engine and all of its bodily fluids had made the 1973 Mk I Ford Capri much lighter, but not light enough to be lifted the necessary three feet to place it on our stage. Not deterred, we built a ramp; which resulted in two members of staff and half a dozen students having to run for their lives or be crushed by a large, rusty death trap.

Eventually, we used common sense and some ropes to pull our version of 'Greased Lightning' up on to the stage. The idea was simple. In the scenes where we needed the great machine, we would push it on and simply remove it at the end of the scene using hidden ropes. It had wheels; what could be easier? Then we realized the scenes in the famous hot rod would not be seen or heard with the car's current design. So, without further thought, we used a metal grinder and a keen technology teacher to remove the roof. It was soon after that that we realized the rear windscreen would also have to be removed as it kind of got in the way. Eventually, having quite sensibly covered the jagged edges of Ford rust and steel with gaffer tape, there it was – freshly sprayed in purple and gold – 'Greased Lightning'. It truly was a sight to behold. Oddly, the scrap yard didn't want it back! I went on to produce *Grease The Musical* another two times, and neither time did I even think of recreating that experience. MDF and paint were cheaper, easier and certainly safer. But people did talk about our first 'Greased Lightning'. They still do.

The Crucible

In every play, there is a moment where, if you get it right, you'll captivate your audience completely. When they're on the edge of their seats, wanting to call out to Romeo, 'Wait, she's about to wake up!' or shout, 'Don't shoot, they're brothers!' That moment when the entire audience silently begs Arthur Kipps not to open the attic door. When an audience responds, on cue and exactly as you intended, it's the best feeling for you and your cast.

Most plays have *that* moment. Often, the cast will discover it in rehearsal and suddenly everything seems to revolve around it. It could be a grand culmination or something subtle and understated, but it's always a powerful exploration of tension. For me, that moment in *The Crucible* comes in Act three, when Abigail and the girls point to the ceiling in the courtroom. There's no yellow bird, yet the entire audience looks up, gripped by shared and palpable fear. That's the magic of theatre: that moment.

After the madness of complex sets and cars, the idea of a simple set was a blessing. I love minimalist sets. More and more as it happens! It was to be a studio performance, so not the large proscenium arch stage of the school hall with its raked seating. The idea of the audience being up close and intimate was perfect for the set I had in mind. I wanted our audience to be in John Proctor's parlour; in that courtroom; in a clearing in the woods. But as directors often do, I wanted something more. I wanted to increase the intimacy and I came up with the idea of steeply raking seating (on modular staging) on three sides so it felt like we (the audience) were looking down into their lives from above. It limited seating to around 50 but it worked and at 'that moment' when Abigail pointed up at the yellow bird, the audience felt it among them. There was a gasp. What more can you ask for!

Oliver!

Mention *Oliver!* in certain circles and folk just break into song; *Consider Yourself* or *Food Glorious Food* spring to mind. The music is memorable, the play unforgettable!

With its large cast and diverse range of characters, including both lead and ensemble roles, it's one of the best for accommodating large student groups. The mix of male and female characters offers many opportunities for casting, particularly with the iconic roles of Oliver, Fagin, Nancy and that ensemble of street kids! It has a strong youth appeal, with central characters like Oliver and the Artful Dodger being young themselves, this story resonates with school-aged performers and the themes of adventure, survival and hope are totally relatable.

It's familiar, based on Charles Dickens's *Oliver Twist*, and follows a well-known, timeless narrative. Many audiences already know the plot, which encourages tickets sales and participation. I love the balance of serious, emotional moments and the light comedic ones, giving students a chance to develop both dramatic and musical/dance theatre skills. It has it all, but the reason I love it so much is down to the sheer challenge and the opportunities for staging and set design. The Victorian London setting provides rich opportunities for creative set and costume design.

Most of the action could take place on the main stage, which would utilize nearly all of its space. But how could I create the other necessary areas? This is where levels became essential! I envisioned a high rooftop for Bill Sikes's dramatic end and a hidden, subterranean den for Fagin and his gang. With scaffolding donated by a parent who owned a building company, we constructed a three-level set extending from the back of the stage.

This design gave us the large main stage area plus two additional levels behind it. The first level, accessible via steps on both stage left and right, served as the funeral parlour and other grim locations. When dimly lit, it transformed into Fagin's hideout. At the centre of this level was a fireplace that cleverly concealed a hidden entrance, allowing the gang to enter from backstage.

The top level, accessible only by a backstage ladder, became a narrow planked walkway designed specifically for Bill Sikes's final scene. To enhance the setting, we used a gobo to project a Dickensian London skyline, which worked brilliantly. For Sikes's six-inch 'fall', we had a safety mat positioned to one side, hidden below a parapet of rooftops.

Positioning the levels at the back kept the wings clear for cast and prop entrances and exits. This set-up provided ample space for large dance and ensemble numbers while also allowing intimate scenes to stand out, defined by the varying levels and lighting.

Warning: scaffolding should only be assembled and checked by a professional, qualified scaffolder.

The Mysteries

I've always been partial to working with levels, so the idea of a promenade performance was a real challenge. I had played Angel Lucifer in the same play during my university days, where we took the production on tour as far as Budapest. Touring teaches you to be minimalist with sets and props, and adaptable to any venue. One night, we'd perform in a large theatre with a vast seated audience and the next, in a university foyer or a small classroom. But the venue that moved me the most was a church. It felt both historically fitting and emotionally powerful, perfectly aligning with the site-specific nature of theatre, which has its roots in the early church in Britain.

I wanted to recreate this experience for my students. However, none of the local churches were willing to accommodate three nights of performances with the pews removed. In the end, we settled on a promenade-style performance. Unlike the National Theatre and my university production, we had the audience seated in the school hall, with the performance space running through the middle and onto the stage. It worked well, and a local priest who attended asked if we could recreate the crucifixion scene from the Passion segment in his church for Easter. During that performance, we staged the crucifixion on the steps of the altar. The soldiers struck the floor with mallets next to the cross, which lay on the ground with the body of Christ, and our audience/congregation wept. Perhaps it was the acoustics, the sanctity of the space, or the power of the reenactment itself, but our simple piece of theatre was elevated in a way I've never witnessed since. Many have told me in the years that followed that the moment has stayed with them. Site-specific theatre is definitely worth considering!

Blue Remembered Hills

Sometimes, it's absolutely fine to copy a production, concept, set or style. I once saw a production of Dennis Potter's *Blue Remembered Hills* that so inspired me. It was the very minimalist set and almost total lack of props which appealed to me. Having studied the play as a performance piece for exam groups, the play was well known to me. I had never considered it as anything other than a TV play, but as an intimate studio performance it gains other dimensions.

The problem, however, was that casting fully grown adults to play the children was intended as an ironic, distancing technique to emphasize the cruelty of children. Therefore, re-casting it with children was in a way denying the very essence of the production. Granted, the students were young adults and not seven-year-olds, but the theme of lost innocence was still a challenge. This is where minimalism and the set came in. Gone was the lavish set of The Forest of Dean, a barn and hidden dens. Our distancing was the set. The only item onstage was a large double mattress. On this the cast jumped, bounced and fought. In fact, the only thing it wasn't, was a mattress. In the final scene, it was lifted and held as the locked doors of the barn where Donald dies in the fire. It fell back with his prone body upon it in the final scene as blackout covered A. E. Housman's poem 'Into my heart an air that kills' There wasn't a dry eye in the house.

Though not a huge, all-singing, all-dancing musical on the big stage – in fact there was a cast of five boys and two girls, with simple lighting and a mattress – nonetheless, it is a production I will always remember for its raw power.

One more thing . . .

Whether it's a large-scale, lavish, whole-school production or a small-cast, intimate, studio performance, it's a school play.

On reflection, the things that give me sleepless nights and restless days have resulted in the most joyful and memorable performances. So, is it worth it? Yes, of course it is.

25

A shout-out for Shakespeare!

In Shakespeare's time, theatre was a hugely popular form of entertainment, drawing large and diverse audiences. They say you could smell the audience, and it wasn't pleasant! The Globe Theatre held up to 3,000 people and, on any given day, thousands attended performances across London. Tickets were affordable, with standing room for the 'groundlings' costing about a penny, making it accessible to most people. Theatre offered a mix of entertainment, socializing and drinking; a break from everyday life. Among the audience walked thieves, prostitutes and poets. Shakespeare's plays – with their blend of action, comedy and universal themes – appealed to all social classes, providing both escapism and reflections on contemporary events.

My commitment to introducing Shakespeare into schools has been a driving force in my career, leading me to dedicate an entire chapter to elucidating both the methodology and the rationale.

In this chapter, I will look at persuasive arguments aimed at convincing students and school administrators of the immense value and joy that bringing Shakespeare to the school stage can create.

The two most common objections to Shakespeare are that the stories feel old and unnecessarily complex and that the language sounds just as dated and hard to understand. It's worth remembering that when Shakespeare wrote his plays, it was for the enjoyment of theatre audiences and to make a living. He probably didn't consider they would still be performed 400 years later, but what of that? Audience enjoyment's the thing, but should it be enjoyable for the performers too? Aye, there's the rub. Perhaps we are a little more highbrow about Shakespeare than he intended.

Putting on a Shakespearean school play offers a unique opportunity for students to explore literature, develop skills, build relationships and create unforgettable experiences that resonate far beyond the final curtain. Shakespeare is often seen as academic, something to be studied in English literature and therefore perhaps best left in the classroom. But the man penned 38 plays and plays are for acting. With the added advantage that students who get up and perform a play are as a result more able to understand, empathize and therefore write about it in their literature exam.

I have directed Shakespeare in schools with all ages; from a sixth form's highly choreographed *Hamlet* using Frantic Assembly as inspiration, to primary school children in Argentina (for whom English is a second language) performing *A Midsummer Night's Dream*. What they and every production in between had in common was that they all started by playing with the text, by having fun with the words and the stories they tell. Simply playing with the play.

To me, *A Midsummer Night's Dream* is an excellent entry point into Shakespeare's works, suitable for beginners right up to professional performances. Its humour and clear structure make it easy to divide into manageable sections, and it offers flexibility – you can approach it as simply or as intricately as desired. The play's versatility is evident, as it is studied by students as young as six, through to university level. What I find most appealing, however, is its universal accessibility. While the plot may seem complex at first, it invites exploration and discovery in a way that resonates with everyone.

Right, so we know why it's a good thing, but how do we convince everyone else to get involved?

Convincing the school

Educational value: Shakespeare's plays are a cornerstone of English literature and provide a rich educational experience. They offer students the opportunity to delve into complex language, themes and characters; enhancing their understanding of literature and improving their analytical skills. It is also excellent for students in the audience, who may be studying a particular text, to see it being performed as intended.

Language and communication: performing Shakespeare helps students develop their language and communication skills. The intricate language of Shakespeare's works requires careful study and practice, which can greatly improve students' vocabulary, pronunciation, and comprehension.

Cultural literacy and transcendent themes: Shakespeare's works are an integral part of our cultural heritage. By participating in a Shakespeare play, students gain a deeper appreciation for the cultural and historical context of the Renaissance period, as well as the timeless relevance of the themes explored in his plays.

Critical thinking: interpreting Shakespeare's texts requires critical thinking and creative interpretation. Students will learn to analyse characters' motivations, explore different themes and consider various directorial choices, fostering their critical thinking and creativity.

Performance skills: performing Shakespeare on stage is a challenging but immensely rewarding experience. It is confidence-building and prepares students well for teamwork and public speaking.

School prestige: a successful Shakespeare production will enhance the school's reputation for excellence in the arts.

Convincing the students

Simply announcing to the students; 'The next school production will be William Shakespeare's *Romeo and Juliet*' may not prompt bustling, eager crowds for audition. Take control and start by introducing key features of the plot, without giving away the title. Before I mentioned *Romeo and Juliet*, I began by placing cryptic posters around the school. A pair of stylized hearts on the drama noticeboard, chalk-outlined bodies on a poster, crossed swords, a balcony etc. It got students talking and guessing; they wanted to know. Once you have them hooked, reel them in.

Fun and challenging: performing a Shakespeare play is not only a great challenge but also a lot of fun. You'll get to explore fascinating characters, complex relationships and exciting plot twists. It's a unique opportunity to push your acting skills to new heights.

Mastering the language: Shakespeare's language may seem tough at first, but learning it is like unlocking a secret code. You'll become more confident in understanding and using complex language, which can help you in all your subjects, not just drama.

Timeless stories: Shakespeare's stories are timeless and universal. They explore themes like love, power, jealousy, and ambition; things that are still relevant today. You'll find yourself connecting with the characters and their struggles in ways you might not expect.

Personal growth: taking on a Shakespearean role will help you grow as an actor and as a person. You'll develop your ability to memorize lines, understand motivations and deliver powerful performances. It's a fantastic way to build confidence and self-discipline.

Teamwork and friendship: putting on a play is a team effort, and working on a Shakespeare production will bring us all closer together. It's something very special.

Impress and inspire: performing Shakespeare is impressive! Your friends, family and teachers will be blown away by what you can achieve. It's an opportunity to inspire others and show what you're capable of.

Lasting memories: being part of a Shakespeare play is an experience you'll remember for the rest of your life. The skills you develop, the friendships you make and the sense of accomplishment you'll feel will stay with you long after the final curtain.

Accessing Shakespeare

Shakespeare's language can be challenging to comprehend and deliver convincingly, yet I have never used 'simplified texts', not with any students, including those for whom English is a second language. Collaborative efforts among actors and directors are essential in dissecting the text, understanding its meaning, and finding effective ways to convey emotions and intentions to the audience; however, I believe too much dissecting is a poor use of time. Simply by performing the lines, listening to the meter and asking the following can be more constructive:

- Where is it?
- Who is there?
- What are they doing?
- What do they want?

Get them on their feet, pointing at the people, objects and even feelings being referred to.

Each line/verse of Shakespeare's can stand alone. You can pull it apart all you like or you can do it and see where it takes you. Such was the genius of the man. His works offer great opportunities for creative interpretation, allowing students to experiment not only with performing but with costume design, set construction and theatrical techniques to bring the text to life in innovative ways.

Getting into the text

Tell them the story so they know who is who, and what they do!

Try some of these simple exercises as a way into the text.

Word emphasis: choose a passage from the text and read it aloud, emphasizing different words each time. Notice how the meaning of the passage changes with each emphasis. This exercise helps in understanding the nuances and layers of meaning in the text.

Character exploration: select a character from the text and research their background, motivations and relationships. Then, act out a monologue or dialogue from the perspective of that character, focusing on embodying their emotions and intentions.

Physicalization: experiment with different physical movements and gestures while delivering your lines. Pay attention to how your body language can enhance or alter the meaning of the text. This exercise helps in conveying emotions and intentions non-verbally.

Walking the lines: take a speech/soliloquy and walk as you speak; each time you think there is a change of mood, change direction or stop at a dilemma before moving in the opposite direction. What does the little dance tell you about the character's state of mind?

Improvise scenes: take a scene from and improvise alternative interpretations or endings. This exercise encourages creativity and helps actors to think outside the box while exploring the text.

Voice work: practise different vocal techniques such as projection, pacing and inflection while delivering your lines. Experiment with variations in tone, pitch and rhythm to bring the text to life.

Contextualization: research the historical and cultural context of the play and its characters. Understanding the societal norms, values and beliefs of Shakespeare's time can provide insights into the motivations and behaviours of the characters.

Scene analysis: analyse the structure and themes of a scene, paying attention to the relationships between characters, the conflicts and the resolutions. This exercise helps in understanding the play as a whole and the significance of each scene.

Most important by far are the words themselves and how they are placed together.

Tell your students about the words and phrases Shakespeare added to our language. He introduced over 1,700 words by changing nouns into verbs, connecting words never before joined, making verbs into adjectives, adding suffixes and prefixes, and so on. In addition to all this, Shakespeare also invented totally new words.

When reading Shakespeare, students will discover words they have never used before or see familiar words used in unusual ways. Yet, even the most unfamiliar words take on a familiar sound when they are performed and heard. Performance often uncovers the written word's meaning.

The key to Shakespeare is to do it. Word patterns and their meanings become apparent in performance. Shakespeare's works are almost completely void of stage direction (save a few famous exceptions). What this means is that a performer must hear the clues within the lines they speak. This is not as complicated as it sounds. Often, the sound of the words will inform the actor how to perform them, both vocally and physically.

Get students to listen. A simple yet effective demonstration of the power of a simple word is to ask students to say 'I love you', then 'I hate you' (both with feeling). Ask the rest of the group how the two words changed the very look of the speaker's face. Think of the open sound of 'love' compared with the closed sound of 'Hate'. Say 'Romeo', 'Benvolio', 'Mercutio'. Now say 'Tybalt'.

Examine the effects of monosyllables, rhyme, onomatopoeia, assonance, alliteration, personification. How do they change the mood and very meaning of a line or scene?

Consider other words and names in the text that are used with the similar result. Bearing in mind the lack of stage directions, what might Shakespeare be telling us about the character, their motivations etc.?

In Chapter 4, 'What's out there?', I offer a separate section for Shakespeare's works with a list giving 10 of the most accessible of his works along with cast sizes and suggested age groups.

Finally, bringing Shakespeare into schools needn't be just about the academic; it's about giving students a real hands-on experience that blends learning with creativity. Yes, Shakespeare can seem tough at first, but the benefits go way beyond simply understanding the text. Students get to sharpen their critical thinking, improve communication, work as a team and connect with timeless stories in a way that's both fun and meaningful.

For me, Shakespeare is all about entertaining and engaging audiences. When students get to play with his works they gain a deeper appreciation of the language and themes, while also building confidence and finding their own unique approach. Making Shakespeare fun and accessible means we're tapping into the true spirit of his plays: lively, engaging and meant for everyone to enjoy.

One more thing . . .

One might wonder, why not explore other classic playwrights such as Ben Jonson, Aphra Behn, Marlowe or even Sophocles? And rightly so; the same reasoning applies to their works.

26

'So, what are we doing next?'

It's a sign of success. You're thinking how wonderful it will be to get your afternoons and evenings back and return to a semblance of normality, but the entire cast and crew just want to know, what's next and when?

They're right of course, you should be planning, but you need to look back in order to plan forward. So, before that.

After completing your first school production as a director, there are several important tasks to handle. Let's have one last list!

Immediate tasks after the show:

- Strike the set: safely dismantle and store set pieces, props, costumes and equipment. Clean and return any rented items (costumes, props, lighting equipment) and ensure nothing is missing or damaged.
- Organize a clean-up with the students, to leave the performance space as you found it (or better).
- Inventory check and storage: take stock of all costumes, props and technical equipment used during the production. Ensure proper labelling and storage for future use.
- Final financials: reconcile all receipts, expenses and income from ticket sales or fundraisers.
- Submit financial reports and ensure any remaining bills are paid.
- Evaluate whether the production met, exceeded or fell short of its budget.
- Thank-you notes: it's quite a bit of work after the madness of the last few months, but try to make time to thank people. Send personalized thank-you notes to anyone who helped with the production, whether they are parents, staff or volunteers; and don't forget any sponsors, if you had them.
- Acknowledge cast and crew with a small celebration (e.g. a cast party, certificates or awards).
- Post-show reflection session; conduct a meeting with cast and crew to celebrate their achievements and share feedback. Encourage students to reflect on what they learned and areas they would like to

improve. Facilitate constructive conversations on teamwork, communication and performance.
- Collect audience feedback: distribute surveys to audience members, or gather informal feedback from parents, staff and students. Ask for comments on pacing, staging, sound, lighting and overall enjoyment. I recommend one of the many online tools such as Google Forms, SurveyMonkey and JotForm, which are excellent tools for gathering feedback whilst offering ease of use, customizable question types and accessible data analysis features.
- Review show recording: watch the recording of the performance with your team to critique blocking, lighting, sound and actor delivery. Use this as a tool to assess both strengths and areas for improvement.

Reflection and feedback for improvement

Student performance evaluation

Assess how well students applied the skills learned during rehearsals.

Identify which acting techniques or strategies were most effective and which need more focus in the next production.

Consider whether the rehearsal schedule was sufficient for the level of performance expected.

Production process review

Reflect on the effectiveness of the production timeline, including rehearsal scheduling, set-building and tech rehearsals.

Evaluate whether communication with the technical team (lighting, sound, set designers) was clear and timely.

Audience engagement

Reflect on audience turnout and engagement. Did marketing efforts reach the intended audience? Were tickets sold as expected?

Consider any suggestions from the audience about performance length, clarity of the storyline, or any technical elements that could be improved.

Teamwork and communication

Analyse the dynamics of the cast and crew. Were there any issues with communication, teamwork, or problem-solving?

Identify leadership moments – both yours and among the students – and note what worked well and what could be more efficient.

Set and technical elements

Evaluate the set design, lighting, sound and costume choices. Were they practical and effective? Was there any feedback on how they could enhance the storytelling?

Consider safety and logistics: were there any issues or concerns during the performances that need addressing in the future?

Student and parent feedback

Hold individual or small-group feedback sessions with students to learn about their experiences; both positive and challenging.

Encourage parent feedback, especially about the process leading up to the show (rehearsal times, communication, ticket pricing etc.).

Teacher reflection

Reflect on your directorial style. What worked well in terms of student direction and motivation? What challenges arose, and how could they be handled differently?

Consider whether you provided enough resources, support and guidance for your students to succeed.

Areas for improvement

Rehearsal efficiency

Were rehearsals organized and productive, or did time management need improvement? Could more be done in fewer rehearsals?

Evaluate the balance between line-learning, blocking and character work.

Tech integration

Was the integration of technical elements (lighting, sound, costumes, props) smooth? Were there any tech-related delays or issues during the show?

Plan for more or better-timed tech rehearsals next time if needed.

Student support and learning

Reflect on whether each student had adequate time to develop their character and gain confidence in their role.

Consider any adjustments in how you coach line memorization, emotional delivery or physicality.

Casting and play selection

Was the chosen play or musical well suited to the cast's abilities? Would a different play have been a better fit for their strengths or interests?

Evaluate casting decisions. Were students given roles that allowed them to grow and showcase their talent?

Marketing and publicity

Was enough done to promote the show to ensure a strong turnout? Were ticket prices appropriate for the community?

By examining these areas, you'll not only figure out what was a hit and what might need a little tweaking. Think of it as fine-tuning for future productions!

One final thing, or two . . .

I realize that I haven't written a specific chapter on the performance nights themselves. Why not? This book focuses on creating a tradition of theatre, of reflection and excellence for you and your students; one that fosters school productions, anticipated with excitement and remembered with fondness.

To achieve this, if I were to choose a single word from my book that encapsulates this goal, it would be: ORGANIZE!

Oh, and me? My favourite show to direct was *Macbeth*. We kept it simple and bloody.

And the best piece of theatre I ever saw was probably *Mother Courage* at the National in 2009. It was epic in every sense, a virtual checklist of every Brechtian technique for my students featuring live music (Duke Special) and vast moving sets. Because you should leave the theatre feeling challenged and changed.

That's all folks! The following pages contain the appendices referred to throughout the book. Feel free to adapt.

APPENDIX A

The one you hand out at the end of the first meeting.

Audition information pack

Thanks for coming to our first meeting for this year's school production! We're excited to have you on board.

About the show

- **Title**: This year, we'll be putting on *[Show Title]*
- **Plot**: Here's a brief summary: *[Plot Description]*
- **Tagline** (if applicable): *[Tagline]*

Performance dates

- The performances will be on: *[Full Date and Day]*
- All shows will start at: *[Time]*
- The show will run for: *[Approximate run time]*

Weekend rehearsals *[if applicable]*

- **Saturday** (tech rehearsal): *[Date and Time]*
- **Sunday** (dress rehearsal): *[Date and Time]*

Rehearsal schedule

You'll get a full rehearsal schedule, and **attendance is required** for every rehearsal you're called to. If you have any unavoidable conflicts, make sure to write them down at the bottom of this form.

Interested in a role?

- If you want to audition for a **performing role**, please fill out **Part A**.
- If you're more interested in a **non-performing role** (like tech or backstage), fill out **Part B**.

Important reminder

Whether you're auditioning for a performing or non-performing role, please remember that not everyone will get a part or the exact role they wanted – but we appreciate your effort and enthusiasm!

Part A: Performing

Audition information

- **Dates, times, and location:** be aware of when and where the auditions will take place.
- **Cast details:** familiarize yourself with available characters and their descriptions.

Audition prep

- **Attire:** if dancing is involved, we'll provide tips on what to wear.
- **Audition pieces:** check which scenes, songs or lines you need to prepare. For musicals, specific songs will be listed for you to learn.

What to expect at the audition

- **Preparation tasks:**
  - Memorize lines (if applicable).
  - Research the characters you are interested in.

Available roles

- A complete list of characters and their descriptions will be provided (here).
- For musicals, let us know if you:
  - Play an instrument (please list).
  - Are a dancer (include style/training).
  - Are a singer (indicate vocal range if known).
  - Or you simply want an acting part (if possible).

Commitment

- Participating in the show requires a time commitment. Here's an overview of the rehearsal schedule:

- **Rehearsal time frame**: approximately **11–16 weeks**.
- **Weeks 1–9**: rehearsals **3–4 days a week, 2–3 hours** per session.
- **Weeks 10–11**: rehearsals increase to **5 days a week**, still 2–3 hours per session.
- **Final weeks (Weeks 12–16)**: **5 days a week**, with longer sessions in the last 2–3 weeks.
- **Additional rehearsals**: expect added rehearsals closer to performance dates; keep weekends flexible.

After the audition

- Once the cast list is posted (details to be announced), all audition participants will be offered a feedback session, regardless of casting outcome.
- **Feedback sessions**: these **one-on-one** sessions with the director will occur about a week after the cast list is published.

Part B: Crew and technical crew

Interview information

- **Dates, times, and location**: check when and where interviews for technical roles will take place! Be sure to sign up.

Available roles

Below is a list of roles for the production, along with the responsibilities and any skills/experience needed. *[You may wish to tailor these to be specific to your show.]*

- **Backstage crew**: responsible for helping during the show with scene changes, moving props, and keeping things organized behind the scenes.
- **Set design and building**: help create the look and feel of the stage! You'll work with a team to design and build the sets for the production.
- **Art work**: if you're artistic, this role involves painting, creating signs, or adding creative details to the set and props.
- **Props**: you'll be in charge of gathering, creating, and managing all the items actors will use on stage.
- **Wardrobe/costume and make-up**: responsible for designing, organizing, and maintaining costumes, as well as helping with hair and make-up for the actors during the show.

- **Lighting:** operate the lighting equipment and help create the mood for each scene by setting up and controlling the lights.
- **Sound:** manage microphones, sound effects and music cues during the performance.
- **Front of house:** greet the audience, check tickets and help with seating. You'll be the face of the production before the show starts!

Be specific when you fill out which role(s) you're interested in and why. Let us know if you have any experience or special skills that could help you in that role.

Commitment

Being part of the crew means you'll be part of the rehearsals and performance preparation. Here's what you can expect for the rehearsal schedule:

- **Rehearsal time frame:** rehearsals will run for about **11–16 weeks**.
- **Weeks 1–9:** rehearsals will be **3–4 days a week**, with each session lasting **2–3 hours**.
- **Weeks 10–11:** rehearsals will increase to **5 days a week**, lasting 2–3 hours.
- **Final weeks (Weeks 12–16):** we'll rehearse **5 days a week**, and some rehearsals may be longer during the last 2–3 weeks.
- **Weekend rehearsals:** there may be weekend rehearsals closer to the performance, especially in the final week. Make sure to keep your weekends flexible!

After the audition/interview

- Once the cast and crew lists are posted (time, place and location will be announced), everyone who applied will be offered a **feedback session,** whether you got a part or not.
- Feedback will be **one-on-one** with the director and will take place about a week after the lists are posted.

Production agreement form

Before you audition, please carefully review the dates listed below. The performance date and the weekend dress and technical rehearsals are **non-negotiable.** If you know of any conflict or potential conflict with these dates, please reconsider auditioning for this production.

Important non-negotiable dates

- Dress and technical rehearsal (weekend): *[Date and Time]*
- Performance night(s): *[Date and Time]*

Your agreement

- I have read and understood the dates above and confirm that I am available to attend all required dates.
  Or
- I have a potential conflict with the following *date(s)* for the following reasons:
  [Provide details here]

Rehearsal commitment

I agree to attend all rehearsals and meetings punctually throughout the preparation period leading up to the show.

Participation interest

- I am interested in the following specific role/character:
  [Specify role/character]
  Reasons for this choice:
  [Provide reasons]
- Other skills/talents:
  [If you would like to demonstrate any skills/abilities you have which you think may be used in the show, please don't be shy. Tell us. You never know!]
- I am willing to be involved in any role (tech/performing):
  [Specify role preference]
  Reasons for this choice:
  [Provide reasons]

Signatures

- Full name and class/tutor group: _____
- Student signature: _____ Date: ___ / ___ / ___

- Parent/carer signature: _____ Date: ____ / ____ / ____

- Form tutor/homeroom teacher signature: _____
  Date: ____ / ____ / ____

Tutor comments

This section is for your tutor to provide any relevant comments about your participation in the production.

APPENDIX B

The show pack

Congratulations on being part of this great team as we prepare for our production of ******** on **/**/**** and any additional dates.

Please read this document thoroughly and sign the attached rehearsal schedule agreement form.

Included in the show pack are the following:

- A calendar showing all relevant dates associated with the show.
- A rehearsal schedule.
- A synopsis of the play, and any historical notes.
- What is expected of each cast/crew member.
- Appendix C: Glossary of technical terms used in the theatre.
- Appendix E: The student guide to successful rehearsing.
- Appendix F: Rehearsal schedule agreement form.
- A list of characters and performers (in alphabetical order).
- A list of crew (in alphabetical order).
- A list of adult/staff involved and their roles.
- Details of communication lines (school app/platform, emails, phone numbers etc.).

APPENDIX C

Glossary of technical terms used in the theatre

Why it's important to know theatre terms

Helps you understand instructions

Knowing theatre words makes it easier to follow directions, like where to stand or when to speak.

Makes moving on stage easier

Words like 'stage left' and 'upstage' help you know where to go and how to move without confusion.

Helps you look professional

Using proper theatre terms shows you're serious about acting and makes you look more professional during rehearsals and performances.

Working with the tech team

Knowing terms about lights, sound, and props helps you work better with the backstage crew and make the show run smoothly.

Keeps you safe

Some phrases, such as 'Clear the stage', 'Heads up' or 'Going dark!' help keep everyone safe by letting you know when something important is happening.

Fixes problems faster

If something goes wrong, knowing the right terms helps everyone solve problems quickly, like changing lighting or where you're standing.

Makes you a better actor

Learning these terms helps you understand acting and theatre better, which can make your performances even stronger.

Knowing your venue

[You may wish to use simple diagrams here]
There are many types of staging and audience seating. Here are the most common examples.

End-on

A traditional audience seating layout where the audience is facing the stage from one direction. This seating is found in an arch theatre.

[Theatre-in-the-round, thrust, traverse proscenium ... List them here with simple descriptions.]

Rake

A raked stage is a slanted stage that is higher at the back and lower at the front, creating depth and perspective on the stage. The angle is known as the rake.

Knowing your space

We will be performing on a *[Your stage type]* stage.

Finding your way around our stage

- Downstage: a position nearer the audience or at the front of the stage. See also upstage.
- Upstage: a position further away from the audience on a proscenium arch or end-on stage.
- Stage left: the left side of the stage from the perspective of the performer facing the audience.
- Stage right: the right side of the stage from the perspective of the performer facing the audience.

To indicate all of these various sections of the stage, your script may use the following abbreviations:

- C: centre stage
- D: downstage

- R: stage right
- L: stage left
- DR: downstage right
- DC: downstage centre
- DL: downstage left
- U: upstage
- UR: upstage right
- UC: upstage centre
- UL: upstage left

Entrances and exits

The timing and manner in which characters enter and leave the stage. For example; exit slowly, UL (upstage left).

General and technical terms

Act	An act in a play is a major division of the overall structure, typically consisting of multiple scenes, where a significant portion of the plot unfolds and characters develop towards a climax or resolution. Not to mention what an actor does on stage!
Acting area	The 'space' in which the actor may move in full view of the audience. Also known as performance space or stage.
Actor	A performer in a play (the term is gender neutral).
Ad lib	Short for the Latin *ad libitum* meaning 'freely.' In the theatre, to *ad lib* means to improvise lines.
Apron	The apron is any part of the stage that extends past arch and into the audience or seating area. See also, ***thrust***.
Arena	Type of stage without a frame or arch separating the stage from the auditorium, in which the audience surrounds the stage area. See also, ***theatre-in-the-round***.
Auditorium	The area of a theatre where the audience sits.
Backcloth (UK)/ Backdrop (USA)	Large painted or printed curtains or cloths hung at the back of the stage to represent scenery. More specifically, a *drop* is a large piece of fabric hung down onto the stage floor and used to cover the back of the stage or to reduce the size of the stage.
Back projection	The projection of images onto a translucent screen (*scrim*) from behind. Often used for projected scenery and special effects.

Backstage	The area behind and around the *stage* where performers and crew prepare for and manage the production. Unseen by audience.
Beat	A momentary pause or delay in which there is a subtle shift in mood, thought/feeling.
Blackout (UK)/ Fade to black (USA)	The sudden or faded extinguishing of all stage lights at the end of a scene or performance.
Blocking	The choreographed movement and positioning of actors on stage during a performance including entrances and exits. See *staging*.
Border	A narrow, horizontal material masking off an area above the stage. A border hides the lighting rig. They can also define the upper limit of the audience's sight line.
Box office	The area of a theatre where tickets are sold to patrons.
Call	A notice to cast and crew of a rehearsal or performance time. Also used as the countdown to a performance provided by stage management. 'This is your 10 minute call.'
Cast	The company of actors/performers in a play.
Cloth	A piece of painted or plain scenic canvas. A backcloth (or backdrop) hangs at the rear of a scene. A floorcloth or stage cloth is a painted canvas sheet placed on the stage to mark out an acting area, or for a particular effect.
Concentration	The actor's *focus*, also known as centring; focusing on being in character, or being in the moment.
Control room (UK)/Booth (USA)	An enclosed, windowed area, usually at the back of the auditorium, used for technical control, sound and/or lights.
Crew	The wonderful team of people who work backstage and everywhere else out of sight silently ensuring everything works smoothly on the physical aspects of a performance.
Crossfade or fade	The gradual transition from one lighting cue to another.
Cue	A signal, often given verbally or through a specific action, that indicates when a particular event, such as an entrance, line, sound effect or lighting change, should occur during a performance.
Curtain call	The moment at the end of a performance when the cast comes forward to acknowledge applause from the audience.
Cyclorama or cyc	A large, curved backdrop used to create the illusion of sky or distant scenery.

Dialogue	Spoken conversations between two or more characters, where they express their thoughts and feelings.
Director	The director's role is to guide and inspire you, shaping your performances and coordinating the creative vision to bring this production play to life on stage.
Dress rehearsal	Usually the final rehearsal before a public performance, during which costumes and make-up are worn.
Flashback	In a non-linear plot, to go back in time to a previous event; a *flash forward* moves the action to a future event.
Flat(s)	A flat piece of painted scenery often consisting of a wooden frame covered with either wood and/or a stretched fabric, usually canvas. Used to create walls or separations on stage.
Fly system	The system of ropes, pulleys, and counterweights used to raise and lower scenery, curtains and even performers above the stage.
Fly tower (UK)/ Grid (USA)	The area above the stage where scenery, lights and curtains are hung.
Focus	Can refer to lighting where it is the adjustment and shaping of light. In acting, it can refer to a performer's *concentration* or how a performer directs the audience's attention to an action or object on stage.
Follow spot or spotlight	A powerful light with a narrow beam used to follow performers on stage.
Footlights	Not used often today. A row of lights at the front of the stage near the floor which illuminates actors from below. See also, *up lights*.
Foyer	The lobby or entrance area of a theatre.
Front of house (FOH)	The public areas of the theatre, strictly including everything in front of the stage. The *front of house manager* oversees staff members who work in this area.
Front of house manager (UK)/ House manager (US)	The person responsible for managing the front-of-house operations, including seating and audience management.
Gaffa, gaff or gaffer's tape	Is a versatile (almost magical), adhesive, fabric-based tape commonly used in the theatre.
Gel/colour filter or filters	Used to modify stage lighting.
Genre	The kind of drama, for example tragedy, comedy, satire, melodrama, musical.

Gesture	Movements made by a performer's body used to convey meaning, attitudes or feelings.
Gobo	A stencil or template placed inside a lighting fixture to create patterns or project images.
Golds	Stage curtains, also known as grand drapes or main curtains. Large, often ornate, they are positioned at the front of the stage and used to conceal the set before and between acts, as well as for grand reveals or curtain calls at the end of performances.
Green room	The area where actors relax/prepare before and after a performance.
House	The area where the audience sits during a performance. In the UK, 'audience' might also be used interchangeably.
House lights	The lights in the auditorium that illuminate the seating area before and after the performance, as well as during intermissions.
Interval (UK)/ Intermission (USA)	A designated break in a play (half-time if you like!) If your show has no interval you should warn your audience in advance.
Legs	Vertical curtains or flats used to hide the wings from view and frame the audience's view of the stage.
Lighting plan (UK/ Lighting plot (USA)	A scaled drawing showing the type, position, focus and purpose of all lighting instruments in a production. Used by the lighting team to install and operate the lighting design.
Lines	What the actors learn and speak on stage during the performance. You may be told to *'learn your lines!'*
Monologue	A lengthy speech by a single character delivered to other characters in a play.
Offstage	All stage areas outside the visible acting area.
Onstage	The acting area of the stage floor.
Orchestra or band	If you are performing a musical this will be the group of musicians who play for you. The term is also used in the theatre to refer to the seating area immediately behind the orchestra.
Patch	The process of connecting audio or lighting equipment to a mixing console or control panel.
Programme (UK)/Playbill (US)	The printed booklet provided to the audience. Contains cast lists and crews. Can give a brief synopsis of the production, provide a space for director's notes, introductions, a word from the head teacher/principal. It

	can also contain sponsored advertising as an extra form of revenue (see Chapter 4).
Prompt	This is what actors get if they forget their lines.
Props (property)	Objects or items used by actors during a performance to enhance the setting or action.
Props manager (UK)/ Props master (USA)	The invaluable person responsible for managing props.
Raked stage	A sloping stage, higher at the back than at the front, to improve visibility for the audience.
Run/run of a show	The period during which a production is performed continuously without interruption. This time is important for many *tech* and *FOH* reasons.
Scenery	The various flats, drops, etc. that are used to create the visual setting(s) for a play.
Scrim	A translucent gauze or curtain. It can be plain or painted. When light is cast on the front of a scrim, it becomes opaque; but if objects behind it are more brightly lit, they will be visible.
Set	It refers to the physical environment or surroundings in which a theatrical performance takes place. It encompasses everything from the backdrop, props, furniture and structures that create the stage's atmosphere and help convey the setting of the play.
Sight lines	The imaginary lines drawn from the farthest seats to the stage. You should be aware of these as they will determine where the action takes place onstage for all of your audience to see. For *crew*, it is also important to know if you are crossing a sight line and becoming visible to the audience. They may be marked on the floor backstage.
Sound designer/ operator or sound techie	The person responsible for designing and operating the sound for a production including sound effects, microphones etc.
Sound desk (UK)/ Soundboard (US)	The console or device used by a sound technician to control and mix audio signals for amplification and reinforcement during a performance.
Soliloquy	A speech in a play where a character speaks their thoughts aloud, usually while alone on stage. It's a moment when the character reveals their innermost feelings, motivations or dilemmas to the audience, providing insight into their mind and driving the plot forward. Different to a ***monologue***.

Smoke	Stage smoke is produced by the vaporization of various oil-based substances.
	Smoke machines or *'foggers'* direct this nontoxic material on stage to create various effects. *Dry ice* is another option.
Stage crew or stagehands	The crew responsible for setting up and operating technical equipment on stage.
Stage door	The entrance at the rear or side of a theatre used by actors, crew, and staff.
Stage make-up	This is make-up used to shape and define actors' facial features as seen on stage. It should be simple. But can if the character requires it be elaborate, including prosthetics such as artificial body parts or features.
Stage manager	The role of the stage manager is to oversee the smooth running of rehearsals and performances. This very important person gives instructions or 'calls' for most things that take place on stage during a live performance. (Not the director.) They are often seen, except by the audience, lurking in the wings or at the back of the house. On the night, the stage manager is The Boss.
Staging	It encompasses a broader range of elements than *blocking*. It refers to the overall presentation and arrangement of the performance, including the set design, lighting, sound and other technical aspects. Staging involves making creative decisions about how to visually and aurally communicate the themes, mood and atmosphere of the play.
Strike	Refers to the process of dismantling and removing the set after a production. In the UK, this process is also referred to as 'get out.'
Tabs	Short for 'tab curtains', are narrow, vertical curtains that flank the sides of the stage. They are often used to mask the *wings* and *offstage* areas from the audience's view, creating a more focused visual frame for the action taking place onstage. Tabs can be used to adjust the width of the stage opening for different set designs or to create different visual effects.
Tech or technical rehearsal	Both terms refer to a rehearsal focused on technical aspects such as lighting, sound, and effects.
Tech rehearsal (UK)/Run-through (USA)	A full rehearsal of the entire production without stopping.

Technical run (UK)/Cue-to-cue (USA)	A rehearsal focusing on technical elements, such as lighting and sound cues. Very often involves a lot of standing about for the actors as they move from scene to scene and from cue to cue without full dialogue, while the tech crew ensure that they are properly lit and heard.
Traverse stage (UK)/Alley stage (USA)	A stage with audience seating on two sides, often used for experimental or immersive productions.
Up lights	A light positioned on the floor (stage). Used to shine up and create dramatic effects or highlighting features of the set.
Wardrobe mistress/master (UK)/Costume designer (USA)	The person responsible for designing, making, acquiring and maintaining costumes.
Wings	The areas to the sides of the stage (offstage) that are out of view of the audience, where actors wait for their cues and props are stored.
XLR Cable	A type of cable commonly used in audio systems for microphones and other sound equipment.
Yoke	A device used to mount and position lighting instruments.

There are many more you may wish to add to this list. Feel free to add or remove and tailor for your specific show.

Younger students for example need only become familiar with a few, perhaps limited to movement on stage.

APPENDIX D

Job descriptions for your production team

I have not included director, producer or musical director, as these will usually be a founder member of the team... You! However, the last on the list is for an assistant.

I have added all the responsibilities that could be assigned to the role but you may wish to omit many of them or divide the jobs among others or yourself. This will also make the role seem slightly less daunting!

Stage manager

Position: Stage manager for [name of school play]
Position: Stage manager
Location: [School name]
Dates: Production run dates from start to finish including performance dates

Overview:

We are seeking *[or desperately need]* a highly organized, proactive and dedicated individual to volunteer as the stage manager for our upcoming school play. This voluntary role is vital for ensuring the smooth operation of the production, from rehearsals through to the final performance. It's a fantastic opportunity for someone passionate about theatre or eager to learn about the role in an educational setting.

Key responsibilities:

Organizing and managing props and set pieces:
Ensuring all props and set pieces are prepared, properly placed and in good condition.
Coordinating set changes and prop handoffs during rehearsals and performances.

Supervising the backstage crew:
Assigning tasks and roles to crew members.
Ensuring that all crew members understand their responsibilities and are properly trained.

Maintaining backstage order and safety:
Keeping the backstage area organized and free of hazards.
Ensuring that all safety protocols are followed.

Communication and coordination:
Acting as the main point of contact between the stage manager and the backstage crew.
Relaying cues and instructions accurately and promptly.

Problem-solving and crisis management:
Quickly addressing and resolving any issues that arise backstage to prevent disruptions to the performance.
Making quick decisions in the event of unexpected problems.

Ensuring timing and efficiency:
Making sure that set changes and prop handoffs are executed smoothly and on time.
Coordinating with the stage manager to keep the production running on schedule.

Managing costumes and quick changes:
Ensuring that costumes are organized and ready for use.
Coordinating quick changes for actors, making sure they are executed efficiently.

Overseeing rehearsal processes:
Managing backstage activities during rehearsals.
Ensuring that the crew and actors are familiar with their backstage roles and responsibilities.

Supporting actors and crew:
Providing support and assistance to actors and crew members as needed.
Ensuring that everyone is prepared and in the right place at the right time.

Documentation and reporting:
Keeping records of prop and set piece placements, quick change details and other relevant information.
Reporting any issues or needs to the stage manager or director.

Qualifications:

Experience: Previous experience in stage management or a related role would be great but there's no substitute for enthusiasm!

Skills: Strong organizational and communication skills, ability to multitask and problem-solving capabilities.

Knowledge: Understanding of theatre production processes and terminology.

Personal attributes: patient and able to remain calm under pressure.

Benefits:
Opportunity to work in a creative and dynamic environment.
Gain valuable experience in theatre production and management.
Make a meaningful impact on students' educational and artistic experiences.
Be a part of a supportive and enthusiastic community.

How to apply: [As you require] I usually say something like; *'please come and chat to me.....'*

We look forward to welcoming a new volunteer to our dedicated team and working together to create an unforgettable production!

Set designer

Position: Set designer for [name of school play]
Position: Set designer
Location: [School name]
Dates: Production run dates from start to finish including performance dates

Overview:

We are looking for *[or desperately need]* a creative, passionate and collaborative individual to volunteer as the set designer for our upcoming school play. This role is essential in bringing a shared vision to life through the design and creation of the set. It's a wonderful opportunity for someone enthusiastic about theatre or interested in learning about set design within an educational environment.

Key responsibilities:

Design concept:
Collaborate with the director to understand and interpret the artistic vision and thematic elements of the play.
Develop a cohesive set design concept that aligns with the overall vision of the production.
Create sketches, models, or digital designs to illustrate the set design ideas.

Planning and budgeting:
Work with the drama department to establish a budget for set construction and materials.
Source materials and props within the allocated budget.
Plan the construction timeline and ensure the set is completed on schedule.

Set construction:
Lead and supervise the set construction process, involving students and other volunteers where possible.
Ensure all set pieces are safe, functional and aesthetically pleasing.
Coordinate with the technical crew for the installation of the set on stage.

Collaboration:
Work closely with the director, stage manager, costume designer and technical team to ensure all aspects of the production are harmoniously integrated.
Attend production meetings and rehearsals as required to provide input and make necessary adjustments to the set design.

Safety and maintenance:
Ensure all set pieces comply with safety regulations and guidelines.
Conduct regular checks and maintenance on the set throughout the rehearsal and performance period.
Be prepared to address any set-related issues that arise during the production.

Qualifications:

Experience: Previous experience in set design or related artistic fields is highly desirable but being a really handy, practical person is the key.

Skills: Design and visualization skills, creativity, attention to detail and problem-solving abilities.

Knowledge: Understanding of set construction techniques, materials and safety protocols.

Personal attributes: Collaborative, reliable, flexible and able to inspire and guide students and volunteers.

Benefits:
Opportunity to work in a creative and dynamic environment.
Gain valuable experience in set design and theatre production.
Make a meaningful impact on students' educational and artistic experiences.
Be part of a supportive and enthusiastic community.

How to apply: [As you require] I usually say something like; *'please come and chat to me. . . . .'*
We look forward to welcoming a new volunteer to our dedicated team and working together to create an unforgettable production!

Set painter/artist

Position: Set artist [name of school play]
Position: Set artist
Location: [School name]
Dates: Production run dates from start to finish including performance dates

Overview:

We are seeking *[or desperately need]* a talented, imaginative and enthusiastic individual to volunteer as the set artist for our upcoming school play. This role is integral in bringing the visual elements of the set to life and ensuring the artistic vision of the production is achieved. It's a fantastic opportunity for someone passionate about theatre and interested in making a creative impact in an educational setting.

Key responsibilities:

Artistic concept:
Collaborate with the director and set designer to understand and interpret a shared artistic vision of the play.
Develop artistic elements that enhance the set design and contribute to the overall aesthetic of the production.
Create sketches, paintings, murals and other visual elements as required.

Painting and decoration:
Paint and decorate set pieces, backdrops and props according to the design concept.
Ensure that all artistic work is cohesive with the play's theme and setting.
Experiment with different techniques and materials to achieve desired effects.

Collaboration and communication:
Work closely with the set designer, director and other members of the production team to ensure artistic consistency.
Attend production meetings and rehearsals as needed to align the artwork with the play's progression.
Provide artistic input and be open to feedback and adjustments.

Material management:
Source and manage art supplies within the allocated budget.
Ensure all materials are safe and appropriate for use in a school setting.
Maintain an organized workspace and take care of all art tools and supplies.

Student involvement:
Engage and mentor students interested in set art, guiding them in techniques and processes.
Foster a creative and inclusive environment where students feel encouraged to contribute artistically.
Supervise and support students during the painting and decorating process.

Safety and maintenance:
Ensure all artistic elements comply with safety regulations and guidelines.
Conduct regular checks and touch-ups on the set artwork throughout the rehearsal and performance period.
Be prepared to address any art-related issues that arise during the production.

Qualifications:

Experience: Previous experience in art, painting, or set decoration is highly desirable.

Skills: Strong artistic and visualization skills, creativity, attention to detail and ability to work collaboratively.

Knowledge: Familiarity with various painting techniques, materials and safety protocols.

Attributes: Creative, reliable, patient and able to inspire and guide students and volunteers.

Benefits:
Opportunity to work in a creative and dynamic environment.
Gain valuable experience in set art and theatre production.
Make a meaningful impact on students' educational and artistic experiences.
Be part of a supportive and enthusiastic community.

How to apply: [As you require] I usually say something like; *'please come and chat to me. . . . .'*

We look forward to welcoming a new volunteer to our dedicated team and working together to create an unforgettable production!

Lighting technician

Position: Lighting technician for [name of school play]
Position: Lighting technician
Location: [School name]
Dates: Production run dates from start to finish including performance dates

Overview:

We are looking for *[or desperately need]* a technically skilled, detail-oriented and enthusiastic individual to volunteer as the lighting technician for our upcoming school play. This role is crucial in creating the mood, atmosphere and visual impact of the production through effective lighting design and operation. It's a great opportunity for someone passionate about theatre and interested in contributing to an educational environment.

Key responsibilities:

Lighting design:
Collaborate with the director to understand the artistic vision and requirements of the play.
Develop a lighting design that enhances the overall production and complements the set and costumes.
Create lighting plots and cue sheets to outline the lighting plan for each scene.

Equipment set-up and operation:
Set up, test and adjust lighting equipment, including spotlights, LED lights and other fixtures.

Program lighting consoles and control systems for rehearsals and performances.
Operate lighting equipment during rehearsals and performances, ensuring cues are executed correctly.

Technical support:
Troubleshoot and resolve any technical issues related to lighting equipment.
Ensure all lighting equipment is safely and securely installed and maintained.
Conduct regular maintenance checks and repairs as needed.

Collaboration and communication:
Work closely with the director, stage manager, set designer and other production team members to ensure cohesive integration of lighting with other production elements.
Attend production meetings and technical rehearsals to coordinate and refine lighting effects.
Provide input and make necessary adjustments based on feedback from the director and other team members.

Student involvement:
Engage and mentor students interested in lighting design and technology.
Foster a collaborative and educational environment where students can learn and participate in the lighting process.
Supervise and support students during set-up, rehearsals and performances.

Health and safety:
Ensure all lighting set-ups comply with health and safety regulations.
Conduct safety checks on all lighting equipment and cabling.
Be prepared to handle any emergencies related to lighting during rehearsals and performances.

Qualifications:
Experience: Previous experience in lighting design or technical theatre is highly desirable.

Skills: Strong technical and problem-solving skills, attention to detail and ability to work under pressure.

Knowledge: Familiarity with lighting equipment, control systems and safety protocols.

Personal Attributes: Reliable, collaborative, patient and able to inspire and guide students and volunteers.

Benefits:
Opportunity to work in a creative and dynamic environment.
Gain valuable experience in lighting design and theatre production.
Make a meaningful impact on students' educational and artistic experiences.
Be part of a supportive and enthusiastic community.

How to apply: [As you require] I usually say something like; *'please come and chat to me. . . . .'*

We look forward to welcoming a new volunteer to our dedicated team and working together to create an unforgettable production!

Sound technician/engineer

Position: Sound engineer/technician for [name of school play]
Position: Sound engineer/technician
Location: [School name]
Dates: Production run dates from start to finish including performance dates

Overview:

We are seeking *[or desperately need]* a technically proficient, detail-oriented and enthusiastic individual to volunteer as the sound engineer/technician for our upcoming school play. This role is essential in ensuring high-quality audio for the production, including music, sound effects and amplification of dialogue. It's an excellent opportunity for someone passionate about theatre and interested in making a significant contribution to an educational setting.

Key responsibilities:

Sound design:
Collaborate with the director to understand the artistic vision and audio requirements of the play.
Develop a sound design that enhances the overall production, including selecting and editing sound effects and music.
Create a sound cue sheet detailing the audio plan for each scene.

Equipment set-up and operation:
Set up and configure sound equipment, including microphones, speakers, mixers and playback devices.
Conduct sound checks and balance audio levels for rehearsals and performances.
Operate sound equipment during rehearsals and performances, ensuring cues are executed accurately.

Technical support:
Troubleshoot and resolve any technical issues related to sound equipment.
Ensure all sound equipment is safely and securely installed and maintained.
Conduct regular maintenance checks and repairs as needed.

Collaboration and communication:
Work closely with the director, stage manager and other production team members to ensure cohesive integration of sound with other production elements.

Attend production meetings and technical rehearsals to coordinate and refine audio effects.
Provide input and make necessary adjustments based on feedback from the director and other team members.

Student involvement:
Engage and mentor students interested in sound design and technology.
Foster a collaborative and educational environment where students can learn and participate in the sound process.
Supervise and support students during set-up, rehearsals and performances.

Health and safety:
Ensure all sound set-ups comply with health and safety regulations.
Conduct safety checks on all sound equipment and cabling.
Be prepared to handle any emergencies related to sound during rehearsals and performances.

Qualifications:

Experience: Previous experience in sound engineering or technical theatre is highly desirable.

Skills: Strong technical and problem-solving skills, attention to detail and ability to work under pressure.

Knowledge: Familiarity with sound equipment, mixing consoles, audio software and safety protocols.

Personal Attributes: Reliable, collaborative, patient and able to inspire and guide students and volunteers.

Benefits:
Opportunity to work in a creative and dynamic environment.
Gain valuable experience in sound engineering and theatre production.
Make a meaningful impact on students' educational and artistic experiences.
Be part of a supportive and enthusiastic community.

How to apply: [As you require] I usually say something like; *'please come and chat to me. . . . .'*

We look forward to welcoming a new volunteer to our dedicated team and working together to create an unforgettable production!

Wardrobe

Position: Wardrobe coordinator for [name of school play]
Position: Wardrobe coordinator
Location: [School name]
Dates: Production run dates from start to finish including performance dates

Overview:

We are seeking *[or desperately need]* a creative, organized and enthusiastic individual to volunteer as the wardrobe coordinator for our upcoming school play. This role is essential in ensuring that all costumes enhance the production's overall visual impact and align with the director's vision. It's a fantastic opportunity for someone passionate about theatre and interested in contributing to an educational environment.

Key responsibilities:

Costume design and selection:
Collaborate with the director to understand the artistic vision and costume requirements of the play.
Design, select or source costumes that reflect the characters and time period of the production.
Create costume plots detailing the costume needs for each character and scene.

Fitting and alterations:
Organize and conduct costume fittings for all cast members.
Make or oversee necessary alterations and adjustments to ensure proper fit and comfort.
Address any costume-related issues that arise during rehearsals and performances.

Maintenance and organization:
Maintain all costumes in good condition, ensuring they are clean, repaired and ready for each performance.
Organize and label costumes for easy identification and quick changes.
Keep a detailed inventory of all costumes and accessories.

Collaboration and communication:
Work closely with the director, stage manager and other production team members to ensure cohesive integration of costumes with other production elements.
Attend production meetings and rehearsals as required to coordinate and refine costume use.
Provide input and make necessary adjustments based on feedback from the director and other team members.

Student involvement:
Engage and mentor students interested in costume design and wardrobe management.
Foster a collaborative and educational environment where students can learn and participate in the wardrobe process.
Supervise and support students during costume fittings, alterations and quick changes.

Health and safety:
Ensure all costumes comply with health and safety regulations.
Conduct safety checks on all costume elements, including footwear and accessories.
Be prepared to handle any costume-related emergencies during rehearsals and performances.

Qualifications:

Experience: Previous experience in costume design, fashion, or wardrobe management is highly desirable.

Skills: Strong sewing and alteration skills, creativity, attention to detail and organizational abilities.

Knowledge: Familiarity with costume design, historical fashion and safety protocols.

Personal Attributes: Creative, reliable, patient and able to inspire and guide students and volunteers.

Benefits:
Opportunity to work in a creative and dynamic environment.
Gain valuable experience in costume design and theatre production.
Make a meaningful impact on students' educational and artistic experiences.
Be part of a supportive and enthusiastic community.

How to apply: [As you require] I usually say something like; *'please come and chat to me. . . . .'*
We look forward to welcoming a new volunteer to our dedicated team and working together to create an unforgettable production!

Make-up

Position: Make-up coordinator for [name of school play]
Position: Make-up and hair coordinator
Location: [School name]
Dates: Production run dates from start to finish including performance dates

Overview:

We are seeking *[or desperately need]* a talented, detail-oriented and enthusiastic individual to volunteer as the make-up and hair/wig coordinator for our upcoming school play. This role is essential in creating the visual appearance of the characters through make-up and hairstyling, enhancing the overall production. It's a wonderful opportunity for someone passionate about theatre and interested in making a creative impact in an educational setting.

Key responsibilities:

Make-up and hair design:
Collaborate with the director to understand the artistic vision and requirements for character appearance.
Develop make-up and hair designs that reflect the characters, time period and themes of the production.
Create face charts and hair/wig styling guides for each character.

Application and styling:
Apply make-up and style hair/wigs for cast members during rehearsals and performances.
Teach and assist cast members with make-up application and hair/wig styling techniques.
Ensure all make-up and hairstyles/wigs are consistent and maintained throughout the performance.

Maintenance and organization:
Maintain make-up kits, hair tools and wigs in good condition, ensuring they are clean, sanitized and organized.
Conduct regular checks and touch-ups on make-up and hairstyles/wigs during rehearsals and performances.
Keep an inventory of all make-up products, hair tools and wigs.

Collaboration and communication:
Work closely with the director, costume designer and other production team members to ensure cohesive integration of make-up and hair with other production elements.
Attend production meetings and rehearsals as required to coordinate and refine make-up and hair designs.
Provide input and make necessary adjustments based on feedback from the director and other team members.

Student involvement:
Engage and mentor students interested in make-up artistry and hairstyling.
Foster a collaborative and educational environment where students can learn and participate in the make-up and hair process.
Supervise and support students during make-up application and hairstyling sessions.

Health and safety:
Ensure all make-up and hair/wig set-ups comply with health and safety regulations.
Conduct safety checks on all make-up products and hair tools, ensuring they are safe for use on skin and hair.
Be prepared to handle any make-up or hair-related emergencies during rehearsals and performances.

Qualifications:

Experience: Previous experience in make-up artistry, hairstyling, or wig maintenance is highly desirable.

Skills: Strong make-up application and hairstyling skills, creativity, attention to detail and organizational abilities.

Knowledge: Familiarity with make-up products, hairstyling techniques, wig maintenance and safety protocols.

Personal attributes: Creative, reliable, patient and able to inspire and guide students and volunteers.

Benefits:
Opportunity to work in a creative and dynamic environment.
Gain valuable experience in make-up artistry and hairstyling for theatre production.
Make a meaningful impact on students' educational and artistic experiences.
Be part of a supportive and enthusiastic community

How to apply: [As you require] I usually say something like; '*please come and chat to me. . . . .*'

We look forward to welcoming a new volunteer to our dedicated team and working together to create an unforgettable production!

Front of house

Position: Front of house manager for [name of school play]
Position: Volunteer front of house manager
Location: [School name], [location]
Dates: Production run dates from start to finish including performance dates

Overview:

We are seeking *[or desperately need]* a friendly, organized and enthusiastic individual to volunteer as the front of house manager for our upcoming school play. This role is crucial in ensuring a positive and smooth experience for our audience members, from the moment they arrive until they leave. It's a fantastic opportunity for someone passionate about theatre and interested in contributing to an educational environment.

Key responsibilities:

Audience management:
Oversee all front of house operations during performances, including ticket sales, ushering and audience seating.
Ensure the lobby and auditorium are welcoming, tidy and accessible to all audience members.

Address any audience concerns or issues promptly and courteously.

Student volunteer coordination:
Recruit, train and supervise front of house volunteers, including ushers and ticket takers.
Create and manage volunteer schedules, ensuring adequate coverage for all performances.
Provide clear instructions and support to volunteers, fostering a positive and collaborative team environment.

Box office management:
Manage the box office, including ticket sales and reservations.
Handle cash transactions and maintain accurate records of ticket sales and receipts.
Provide box office reports to the production team as required.

Pre-show preparation:
Ensure all promotional materials, programmes and signage are prepared and displayed appropriately.
Coordinate with the director and production team to confirm all front of house procedures align with the overall production plan.
Conduct pre-show briefings for volunteers to ensure everyone is informed and prepared.

Health and safety:
Ensure all front of house operations comply with health and safety regulations.
Monitor audience areas for any potential hazards and address them promptly.
Be prepared to handle any emergencies, including evacuations if necessary.

Post-show duties:
Oversee the clean-up and organization of the lobby and auditorium after each performance.
Gather feedback from audience members and volunteers to improve future front of house operations.
Prepare a summary report of front of house activities for the production team.

Qualifications:

Experience: Previous experience in customer service, event management or theatre front of house operations is highly desirable.

Skills: Strong organizational and communication skills, ability to manage a team and excellent interpersonal skills.

Knowledge: Familiarity with box office systems, ticketing processes, and health and safety protocols.

Personal attributes: Friendly, reliable, patient and able to remain calm under pressure.

Benefits:
Opportunity to work in a creative and dynamic environment.
Gain valuable experience in event management and theatre operations.
Make a meaningful impact on the audience's experience and the success of the production.
Be part of a supportive and enthusiastic community

How to apply: [As you require] I usually say something like; *'please come and chat to me. . . . .'*

We look forward to welcoming a new volunteer to our dedicated team and working together to create an unforgettable production!

Choreographer

Position: Choreographer for [name of school musical]
Position: Choreographer
Location: [School name]
Dates: Production run dates from start to finish including performance dates

Overview:

We are seeking *[or desperately need]* a creative, energetic and enthusiastic individual to volunteer as the choreographer for our upcoming school musical. This role is essential in creating and teaching the dance routines and movements that bring the musical to life. It's a wonderful opportunity for someone passionate about dance and theatre, and interested in making a significant impact in an educational environment.

Key responsibilities:

Choreography design:
Collaborate with the director/musical director to understand the artistic vision and requirements of the musical.
Develop and design choreography that enhances the story, characters and overall production.
Create detailed dance routines that align with the music and themes of the show.

Teaching and rehearsing:
Teach choreography to the cast during rehearsals, ensuring all performers understand their movements and cues.
Break down complex routines into manageable sections for easier learning.
Conduct regular rehearsals to refine and perfect the choreography.

Performance preparation:
Ensure all dance routines are performance-ready and polished by the final rehearsals.
Coordinate with the director, musical director and other production team members to integrate choreography seamlessly with other elements of the show.
Attend all technical and dress rehearsals to make necessary adjustments and ensure smooth execution.

Student involvement:
Engage and mentor students interested in dance and choreography.
Foster a collaborative and supportive environment where students feel confident and inspired to perform.
Encourage and guide students to develop their dance skills and stage presence.

Health and safety:
Ensure all choreography is safe and appropriate for the cast, taking into account their skill levels and physical abilities.
Conduct warm-ups and cool-downs to prevent injuries.
Be prepared to address any dance-related injuries or issues that arise during rehearsals and performances.

Administrative duties:
Maintain detailed records of choreography notes, rehearsal schedules and progress.
Communicate regularly with the director and production team to provide updates and receive feedback.
Assist with any additional tasks related to the dance aspects of the production.

Qualifications:

Experience: Previous experience in choreography, dance instruction, or theatre production is highly desirable.

Skills: Strong choreography and teaching skills, creativity, attention to detail and ability to work collaboratively.

Knowledge: Familiarity with various dance styles, musical theatre and stage movement.

Personal attributes: Energetic, patient, reliable and able to inspire and motivate students.

Benefits:
Opportunity to work in a creative and dynamic environment.
Gain valuable experience in choreography and theatre production.
Make a meaningful impact on students' educational and artistic experiences.
Be part of a supportive and enthusiastic community.

How to apply: [As you require] I usually say something like; '*please come and chat to me. . . . .*'

We look forward to welcoming a new volunteer to our dedicated team and working together to create an unforgettable production!

Assistant director (student)

Position: Assistant to the director for [name of school play]
Location: [School name]
Dates: Production run dates from start to finish, including performance dates

Overview:

I am looking for a highly motivated, responsible and enthusiastic student to volunteer as the assistant to the director for our upcoming school play. This vital role offers a fantastic opportunity to gain first-hand experience in directing and the creative process behind a theatre production. Whether you're looking to develop your leadership skills or eager to learn more about the world of theatre, this is an exciting position for you!

Please note this is a very demanding role and would exclude you from being a member of the cast as well.

Key responsibilities:

Supporting the director:

- Assisting the director in the day-to-day management of rehearsals and the overall creative vision of the play.
- Helping to implement directorial decisions, providing input when required, and maintaining the director's vision throughout the production.

Communication and coordination:

- Relaying key information to actors, crew members and other production staff.
- Ensuring that everyone is aware of rehearsal schedules, blocking notes and performance expectations.

Rehearsal management:

- Assisting in organizing rehearsal schedules and making sure all cast and crew are where they need to be at the right time.
- Helping to run rehearsals by cueing actors, helping with blocking, and keeping track of rehearsal notes.

Actor support:

- Providing support and guidance to actors as needed, helping them understand direction and character development.
- Assisting in tracking actor progress and helping the director with any adjustments.

Assisting with set and props:

- Helping the director and production team with the organization of props, costumes and set pieces.
- Ensuring that props are in place for rehearsals and performances, and assisting in set changes as needed.

Problem-solving and crisis management:

- Supporting the director in handling unexpected challenges during rehearsals and performances.
- Ensuring that rehearsals run smoothly by proactively addressing potential issues.

Supporting the creative team:

- Assisting with costume, lighting, sound and set design, ensuring all elements of the production come together cohesively.
- Helping to manage transitions between scenes during rehearsals and performances.

Documentation and reporting:

- Keeping track of rehearsal notes, blocking diagrams and any other necessary documents for the production.
- Reporting any issues or concerns to the director or stage manager promptly.

Qualifications:

- **Experience:** Previous experience in theatre or a passion for learning about directing is ideal but not essential.
- **Skills:** Strong communication and organizational skills, attention to detail and the ability to multitask.
- **Personal attributes:** Responsible, enthusiastic, able to take initiative and work well under pressure.
- **Desirable:** A strong interest in theatre and a desire to learn more about the creative process.

Benefits:

- Opportunity to gain hands-on experience working alongside the director and production team.
- Learn valuable skills in theatre direction, coordination and team management.
- Contribute to creating a memorable and exciting performance for the school community.
- Be part of a creative and supportive team of students and staff.

How to apply:
Please come and chat with me or email [contact information] for more details. We're excited to welcome a motivated student into our team and work together to create an amazing production!

We look forward to welcoming a new volunteer to our dedicated team and working together to create an unforgettable production!

Assistant musical director (student)

Assistant to the musical director (student)
Position: Assistant to the musical director for [Name of School Musical]
Location: [School name]
Dates: Production run dates from start to finish, including performance dates

Overview:

We are looking for a dedicated, organized and enthusiastic student to volunteer as the Assistant to the musical director for our upcoming school musical. This position provides a unique opportunity to gain valuable insights into the musical direction process and to support the team responsible for the production's musical elements. If you have a passion for music and an interest in learning more about theatre production, this role is perfect for you!

Note: This role is demanding and would prevent participation as a cast member or musician.

Key responsibilities:

Supporting the musical director:

- Assist the musical director in coordinating rehearsals, ensuring each session runs smoothly and follows the musical vision.
- Help reinforce directorial decisions regarding musical interpretation and assist with musical elements as needed.

Communication and coordination:

- Serve as a point of contact between the musical director, cast and crew, ensuring clear communication of schedules, updates and music-related details.
- Provide cast members with copies of sheet music, notes and recordings.

Rehearsal management:

- Help organize and manage rehearsal schedules, ensuring cast members are prepared and present for vocal and music practice.
- Support the musical director by cueing cast members, tracking rehearsal progress and managing sheet music and vocal parts.

Cast and vocal support:

- Assist cast members with vocal warm-ups, provide guidance on vocal parts and support their understanding of musical direction.
- Help monitor cast progress in learning songs, harmonies and vocal techniques.

Instrumental and accompaniment coordination:

- Support coordination with instrumentalists or accompaniment, ensuring they have necessary scores, instructions and cues.
- Help manage rehearsals with instrumentalists and vocalists to ensure smooth transitions and balanced sound.

Problem-solving and crisis management:

- Assist in handling any musical challenges that arise during rehearsals or performances, including technical issues with instruments or sound equipment.
- Act proactively to address potential issues that may impact the musical aspects of rehearsals.

Supporting the creative team:

- Coordinate with other production team members to ensure that music cues and transitions are consistent with lighting, staging and choreography.
- Support the musical director in ensuring that all musical elements align with the production's overall vision.

Documentation and reporting:

- Maintain records of rehearsal notes, vocal parts and other essential documents for the musical component.

- Report any concerns, issues or updates to the musical director or stage manager promptly.

Qualifications:

- **Experience:** Previous musical experience or an interest in learning more about musical direction is ideal but not required.
- **Skills:** Strong communication, organization and multitasking skills; musical knowledge (e.g. reading sheet music) is helpful.
- **Attributes:** Responsible, proactive, enthusiastic and capable of working well under pressure.
- **Desirable:** A passion for music, theatre and the creative process of musical production.

Benefits:

- Gain hands-on experience in musical direction and coordination alongside the musical director and production team.
- Learn valuable skills in music direction, teamwork and rehearsal management.
- Contribute to creating a memorable and professional-quality performance for the school community.
- Become part of a creative and supportive team of students and staff.

How to apply:

Please come and chat with me or email [contact information] for more details. We're excited to welcome a motivated student into our team to help bring this musical production to life!

We look forward to making this musical a success together!

APPENDIX E

The student guide to successful rehearsing

[To be included in the show pack. There is a separate sheet for crew]

Dear cast,
Please read and follow these rehearsal tips to help ensure a successful rehearsal and production for cast and crew.

1. You are an important part of rehearsals; without you they will not work! So please check when you are required and be punctual. Arriving on time for rehearsals maximizes the time we have. Punctuality helps set a professional atmosphere and ensures everyone gets the most out of rehearsals.
2. Come prepared by learning your lines and cues as soon as possible. This will save time and allow rehearsals to focus on refining performance aspects, rather than learning basic elements.
3. During rehearsals, stay focused on the task at hand. Minimize distractions such as phones or side conversations to maintain a productive atmosphere.
4. Pay attention to directions from the director and feedback from fellow cast members. Active listening promotes collaboration and helps improve the overall quality of the performance.
5. Use rehearsals as an opportunity to explore different ways of portraying your character. Experiment with voice, gestures and body language to find what works best for your role.
6. Work on stage movements and blocking to ensure smooth transitions between scenes. Practice spatial awareness to avoid collisions and ensure everyone knows their positions on stage.
7. Develop rapport with your fellow cast members to enhance onstage chemistry. Building relationships offstage can translate into more authentic performances onstage.
8. Warm up your voice and stretch your body before rehearsals, to prevent strain and injury. Stay hydrated and avoid shouting or straining your voice unnecessarily.

9 Be open to feedback from the director and fellow cast members, and provide feedback in a constructive manner. Use feedback as a tool for improvement rather than as criticism.

10 Stay positive and enthusiastic throughout the rehearsal process. A positive attitude fosters a supportive environment and encourages creativity and collaboration among the cast and crew.

11 If, for any reason, you know you are going to miss or be late for a rehearsal, please be sure to notify the director (or designated person) as soon as possible.

Dear crew,

Please read and follow these rehearsal tips to help ensure a successful rehearsal and production for cast and crew.

1 You are an important part of rehearsals; without you they will not work! So please check when you are required and be punctual. Arriving on time for rehearsals maximizes the time we have. Punctuality helps set a professional atmosphere and ensures everyone gets the most out of rehearsals.

2 Come prepared by being familiar with the script and what is expected of you.

3 During rehearsals, stay focused on the task at hand. Minimize distractions such as phones or side conversations to maintain a productive atmosphere.

4 Pay attention to directions from the director/stage manager and feedback from fellow crew and cast members. Active listening promotes collaboration and helps improve the overall quality of the performance.

5 Join in all warm-up exercises with cast and crew together. You are an important part of this project and need to look after yourself.

6 Be open to feedback from the director and fellow cast members, and provide feedback in a constructive manner. Use feedback as a tool for improvement rather than as criticism.

7 Stay positive and enthusiastic throughout rehearsals. A positive attitude fosters a supportive environment and encourages creativity and collaboration among the cast and crew.

8 If you operate technical equipment, get to know it well and how to use it effectively and safely. Be attentive, take notes and learn all cues.

9 If you are backstage crew, note where each prop needs to be placed and ensure it is there on time. Be present at all rehearsals you are called for to see how props are used.

10 Pay attention to small details that can make a big difference in the overall production.
11 Be ready to adapt to last-minute changes and challenges.
12 If, for any reason, you know you are going to miss or be late for a rehearsal please be sure to notify the director (or designated person) as soon as possible.

APPENDIX F

Rehearsal schedule agreement form/contract

Congratulations! You have been selected for the part/role of ………………… in our upcoming production of ……………………… on ……/……/……

Remember, you are a vital part of every rehearsal you are called for. Without you, they will not work! Please check when you are required and be punctual. Arriving on time for rehearsals maximizes the time we have. Punctuality is professional and ensures everyone gets the most out of rehearsals.

Come prepared by learning your lines and cues as soon as possible. This will save time and allow rehearsals to focus on refining performance aspects rather than learning basic elements.

During rehearsals, stay focused on the task at hand. Minimize distractions such as phones or side conversations to maintain a productive atmosphere.

Pay attention to directions from the director and feedback from fellow cast members. Active listening promotes collaboration and helps improve the overall quality of the performance.
Phones should be on silent during rehearsals.

Attach the completed (as much as possible) rehearsal schedule.

I have read the attached final rehearsal schedule and confirm I will be able to make all rehearsals promptly.

Signed (student)………………………………X

I/we have read the attached rehearsal schedule and confirm my son/daughter will be able to attend all rehearsals other than any I/we indicated otherwise on the audition form.

Signed (parent/guardian) ………………………X

APPENDIX G

School production risk assessment

A typical risk assessment for producing a school play involves identifying potential hazards, evaluating the risks associated with those hazards, and implementing measures to mitigate them. You know your venue/school and students but this is a basic outline of what a risk assessment for a school play might include:

(See separate assessment for costume and make-up)

1. Introduction

Goal: Ensure the safety of students, staff and the audience during all phases of the school play, including rehearsals, set construction, technical set-ups and performances.

Scope: This covers all activities related to the play, from handling props and costumes to technical set-ups and audience management.

2. Identifying hazards

Physical hazards:

Set construction: Be careful with tools, materials and working at heights. Make sure the stage is solid, and set pieces are stable. Watch out for sharp edges and tripping hazards.

Props and costumes: Ensure props are placed safely, and costumes fit properly to avoid accidents. Be mindful of materials that may catch fire easily.

Stage movement: Falls or collisions can happen during quick scene changes or complex choreography: plan carefully.

Technical hazards:

Lighting and sound: Electrical equipment and cables can pose risks, so ensure everything is set up properly and maintained.

Volume levels: Keep sound levels safe to prevent hearing damage.

Health hazards:

Fatigue: Long rehearsals can lead to tiredness, so balance work with breaks.

Illness/injury: Be mindful of anyone who is unwell or injured. Don't push physical limits during rehearsals.

Mental health: In a school play, student responsibilities should be balanced to avoid undue stress. Assign tasks based on capacity, ensure workloads are manageable, and offer support through regular check-ins. Promoting teamwork helps share tasks and fosters a positive, collaborative experience.

Environmental hazards:

Fire safety: Make sure fire exits, extinguishers and emergency plans are clear and practiced.

Outdoor performances: For outdoor shows, be ready for rain, wind, or extreme temperatures.

Audience safety:

Seating: Prevent overcrowding, keep aisles clear and ensure emergency exits are easy to reach. All seating should be securely fixed and safe.

3. Assess the risks

Severity: How serious could the hazard be? (e.g. minor injury, serious injury, life-threatening)

Likelihood: How likely is the hazard to happen? (e.g. unlikely, possible, likely)

Risk rating: Combine severity and likelihood to give each hazard a rating (e.g. low, medium, high).

4. Implementing safety measures

For physical hazards:

Train students properly on set construction and prop handling.
Use non-flammable materials and make sure costumes are safe and well fitted.
Mark stage edges and other hazards with bright tape.

For technical hazards:

Regularly check all electrical equipment, and have trained staff handle lighting, sound and any special effects.
Control sound levels to prevent hearing damage.

For health hazards:

Schedule regular breaks, and monitor the health of everyone involved. Make sure there is easy access to water, first aid and rest.

For environmental hazards:

Practise fire drills and make sure everyone knows the emergency plan. Have a plan in place for bad weather if the performance is outdoors.

For audience safety:

Arrange seating carefully to avoid overcrowding, keep aisles clear and ensure easy access to exits in case of an emergency.

5. Monitor and review

Supervision: Ensure adults are always supervising during rehearsals and performances.

Regular checks: Continuously assess risks throughout the production.

Feedback: Collect feedback after the show to improve safety for future performances.

6. Keeping records

Documentation: Keep detailed notes on identified risks, safety measures and any incidents.

Emergency procedures: Have clear evacuation plans and a list of emergency contacts (fire, police, medical).

7. Training and communication

Safety briefings: Go over safety protocols with the cast and crew, making sure everyone understands their role in keeping the production safe.

Reporting: Set up a system for reporting hazards or accidents, and deal with them quickly.

8. Legal and insurance considerations

Permissions: Get any necessary permissions for special effects or other activities, and ensure all participants have signed consent forms.

Insurance: Confirm that the school's insurance covers the production, including accidents or damages.

9. Final Approval

Sign-off: The risk assessment should be reviewed and approved by the school's safety officer or a responsible authority.

Costume and make-up often require a specific risk assessment. The person in charge of wardrobe and make-up should at least be aware of the following.

1. Introduction

Objective: Keep students and staff safe when working with costumes and make-up for the school show.

Scope: This covers everything from selecting, fitting and using costumes and make-up, to their storage, application and removal.

2. Identifying hazards

Costume hazards:

Flammability: Costumes made from materials that could catch fire.

Tripping and falling: Long, loose, or ill-fitting costumes may cause trips or falls.

Allergies: Some students may be allergic to costume materials or accessories.

Restricted movement: Tight or restrictive costumes may cause discomfort or injury.

Make-up hazards:

Allergic reactions: Make-up might cause skin or breathing issues, especially if it contains allergens.

Eye injuries: Applying make-up near the eyes can cause irritation or injury.

Hygiene: Sharing make-up or tools could lead to cross-contamination and infection.

3. Assess the risks

Costume hazards: Flammable materials and allergies could lead to serious injury, while tripping hazards could cause anything from minor to more serious injuries.

Make-up hazards: Allergic reactions can range from mild irritation to more serious problems. Eye injuries could also be moderate to serious.

Likelihood

Costumes: Flammable materials or tripping risks are possible if costumes aren't properly checked.

Make-up: Allergic reactions and hygiene issues could occur if individual sensitivities aren't identified, or if make-up isn't handled correctly.

Risk rating: Medium to high for flammability and allergies, medium for tripping and hygiene concerns.

4. Safety measures

Costume safety

Flammability: Use flame-retardant materials and avoid easily flammable fabrics like untreated cotton or synthetic blends.

Fitting: Ensure costumes fit well. Hem long ones and avoid overly loose or tight designs.

Allergy management: Identify allergies in advance and use hypoallergenic materials. Avoid accessories that could trigger reactions.

Movement: Test costumes during rehearsals to make sure they allow free and safe movement.

Make-up safety:

Allergies: Use hypoallergenic, fragrance-free make-up, and do patch tests before applying full make-up, especially for those with sensitive skin.

Application: Teach students or staff safe techniques for applying make-up, especially around the eyes. Keep applicators clean and avoid sharing them.

Hygiene: Provide individual make-up kits if possible. If sharing, use disposable applicators and sanitize regularly.

Storage: Store make-up in a cool, dry place to keep it safe and clean.

5. Monitoring and reviewing

Supervision: Have responsible adults supervise costume fittings and make-up application.

Regular checks: Continuously check costumes for fit and make-up for hygiene.

Feedback: Ask students and staff for feedback on any discomfort or problems with costumes or make-up and adjust accordingly.

6. Documentation

Records: Keep records of allergies, incidents and the safety measures taken.

Emergency procedures: Have a first-aid kit ready during costume fittings and make-up sessions. Know how to respond to allergic reactions or injuries.

7. Training and communication

Briefing: Explain the importance of safety in costume and make-up to students. Show them how to report issues and what to do in case of an emergency.

Reporting: Set up a clear way for students to report any costume or make-up-related problems.

8. Final approval

Sign-off: Have the risk assessment reviewed and approved by the school's safety officer or another responsible authority.

Make-up hazards: Allergic reactions can range from mild irritation to more serious problems. Eye injuries could also be moderate to serious.

Likelihood

Costumes: Flammable materials or tripping risks are possible if costumes aren't properly checked.

Make-up: Allergic reactions and hygiene issues could occur if individual sensitivities aren't identified, or if make-up isn't handled correctly.

Risk rating: Medium to high for flammability and allergies, medium for tripping and hygiene concerns.

4. Safety measures

Costume safety

Flammability: Use flame-retardant materials and avoid easily flammable fabrics like untreated cotton or synthetic blends.

Fitting: Ensure costumes fit well. Hem long ones and avoid overly loose or tight designs.

Allergy management: Identify allergies in advance and use hypoallergenic materials. Avoid accessories that could trigger reactions.

Movement: Test costumes during rehearsals to make sure they allow free and safe movement.

Make-up safety:

Allergies: Use hypoallergenic, fragrance-free make-up, and do patch tests before applying full make-up, especially for those with sensitive skin.

Application: Teach students or staff safe techniques for applying make-up, especially around the eyes. Keep applicators clean and avoid sharing them.

Hygiene: Provide individual make-up kits if possible. If sharing, use disposable applicators and sanitize regularly.

Storage: Store make-up in a cool, dry place to keep it safe and clean.

5. Monitoring and reviewing

Supervision: Have responsible adults supervise costume fittings and make-up application.

Regular checks: Continuously check costumes for fit and make-up for hygiene.

Feedback: Ask students and staff for feedback on any discomfort or problems with costumes or make-up and adjust accordingly.

6. Documentation

Records: Keep records of allergies, incidents and the safety measures taken.

Emergency procedures: Have a first-aid kit ready during costume fittings and make-up sessions. Know how to respond to allergic reactions or injuries.

7. Training and communication

Briefing: Explain the importance of safety in costume and make-up to students. Show them how to report issues and what to do in case of an emergency.

Reporting: Set up a clear way for students to report any costume or make-up-related problems.

8. Final approval

Sign-off: Have the risk assessment reviewed and approved by the school's safety officer or another responsible authority.